BRIGI

FAR FROM THE MADDING CROWD BY THOMAS HARDY

Intelligent Education

Nashville, Tennessee

BRIGHT NOTES: Far from the Madding Crowd
www.BrightNotes.com

ISBN: 978-1-645424-84-0 (Paperback)
ISBN: 978-1-645424-85-7 (eBook)

Published in accordance with the U.S. Copyright Office Orphan Works and Mass Digitization report of the register of copyrights, June 2015.

Originally published by Monarch Press.
Elizabeth R. Nelson, 1966
2019 Edition published by Influence Publishers.

Interior design by Lapiz Digital Services. Cover Design by Thinkpen Designs.

Printed in the United States of America.

Library of Congress Cataloging-in-Publication Data forthcoming.
Names: Intelligent Education
Title: BRIGHT NOTES: Far from the Madding Crowd
Subject: STU004000 STUDY AIDS / Book Notes

CONTENTS

INTRODUCTION TO THOMAS HARDY

BACKGROUND

Although Thomas Hardy was born into Victorian England, and is always considered a Victorian novelist, he shares a common interest with some twentieth century novelists. Like D. H. Lawrence, Ford Madox Ford and E. M. Forster, he is fascinated by England's past and her rural areas. The name "Wessex," as he himself explains, was taken from an old English history; he gave it to a district that was once part of an Anglo-Saxon kingdom.

He was born in this district, in Higher Brockhampton, near Dorchester (Casterbridge, in his novels), on June 2, 1840. Since he was a sickly child, he received his early education at home from his mother, who inspired his love of the classics. His father, a builder and contractor, gave him an early interest in architecture.

When he was about eight years old, he started school in Dorchester. His walk to school took him along country lanes, and he became familiar with rustic scenes. He continued school there until he was about sixteen, when he was apprenticed in the office of John Hicks, a Dorchester architect. He devoted much of his spare time during the years he worked here to his studies of the classics. In 1862, he went to London to work under a

London architect, Arthur Blomfield. He continued his studies of the classics in London, both privately and by attending lectures at Kings College. In 1867, he returned to Dorchester to work with Hicks in restoring churches.

LITERARY CAREER

While he lived in London, Hardy became interested in literature as a possible career. He wrote several poems and some essays, as well as a novel, *The Poor Man* and *the Lady* (1868). The novel was rejected by publishers and destroyed. George Meredith, already established as a novelist, advised Hardy not to write social **satire**, but to try to write a novel with a highly complicated plot. The acceptance of *Desperate Remedies* (1871), which was published anonymously, launched Hardy's career as a novelist. Another novel, *A Pair of Blue Eyes* (1872), was also published anonymously, but Hardy did not achieve literary success until the publication of *Far From the Madding Crowd* (1874). That same year he married Emma Gifford, whom he had met while restoring a church in Cornwall. He and his wife eventually settled at Max Gate, Dorchester, where Hardy spent the remainder of his long life.

LATER LIFE

At Dorchester, he wrote his major novels, including: *Return of the Native* (1878), *Mayor of Casterbridge* (1886), *Tess of the d'Urbervilles* (1891), and *Jude the Obscure* (1895). The novels were usually serialized in magazines before their first publication. The "controversial" subject matter of his books upset Victorian readers, and Hardy reacted by abandoning the novel form. He devoted his later years to writing short stories and poems (particularly, *Dynasts: A Drama of the Napoleonic Wars*, which was published in three parts, in 1904, 1906 and 1908).

In 1912, his first wife died, ending a rather difficult marriage. He married Florence Dugdale in 1914; she survived him and wrote one of the most important Hardy biographies. He died on January 11, 1928, and his ashes were buried in Westminster Abbey.

INTEREST IN NATURE

In most of the Wessex novels, nature is pictured as a hard, unrelenting force. Eustacia and Wildeve (in *Return of the Native*) are not sympathetic to nature, and are eventually destroyed by drowning. Some of this harshness can also be found in *Far From the Madding Crowd*, in scenes such as the one in which the storm threatens Bathsheba's wheat and barley, and in the death of Gabriel Oak's lambs.

The major impact of nature in this novel, however, is of a happier tone. The descriptions include views of nature at its prime: warm spring and summer days spent in sheep washing and shearing, and cold winter nights when the stars are at their brightest. The descriptions are not included only for their beauty; they are integral since they set the atmosphere, and should not be skipped over, as if they were in the way of the plot development.

Hardy's perception of the world of nature is very accurate; small details, like the buttercups which stain Boldwood's boots as he walks through a field on a spring day, show us how wide-awake Hardy's senses were to external impressions of nature.

Moreover, the novel contains Hardy's most complete picture of farm life. To be sure, this life is not always easy, but it provides for happy times at the malthouse, and feasts after sheep shearing. Rural England is at its best here, and some of the atmosphere of older pastorals can be found in Gabriel's characterization, occupation and closeness to nature. When he plays his flute, the world of Sir Philip Sidney's Arcadia is not far off.

WESSEX

With the selection of Wessex as the setting for his novels, Hardy assured his success as a novelist. The area, familiar to him from his childhood, can be located on a modern map. The Anglo-Saxon kingdom includes those southern counties from Surrey in the east, to the Bristol Channel and the Devonshire-Cornwall border on the west. It is rich in legend and the history of England, including its Celtic, Roman, Saxon and medieval past. (Stonehenge, with its mysterious stone ruins and the gigantic earthworks of Maiden's Castle near Dorchester, lie within its boundaries.) Hardy's Wessex is generally confined to the area of Dorsetshire.

It was more than just a physical location for him, however; he prized the economic and social order it had represented, as well as the manners and customs that formed a part of that order. He mourned the passing of these native customs and the changing character of the villages during England's rapid industrialization. He found a way to preserve the old order by capturing it in his novels.

Although the dialect he created for his rustic characters was more often "literary" than accurate, it does convey the simplicity, common sense and humor associated with the natives of this region. The value that these rustic characters placed on the past is sensed in the frequent anecdotes (such as those indulged in by the ancient malster in *Far From the Madding Crowd*). Hardy's retreat to the privacy of Max Gate is almost symbolic of his choice of the past greatness of rural England as the focal point of his work.

FAR FROM THE MADDING CROWD

The title was taken from the familiar, "**Elegy** Written in a Country Churchyard," by Thomas Gray, the eighteenth-century poet. The poem describes the burial of the country people who lived "Far from the madding crowd's ignoble strife." The title serves as an apt, though sometimes ironic, commentary on the novel.

The novel was a result of a request by Leslie Stephens, editor of the *Cornhill magazine*, for a serial. It appeared anonymously in *Cornhill's* in 1874. It was first attributed to George Eliot, much to Hardy's annoyance. It can almost be termed "a novel of setting," since the rural life it describes forms the essence of the novel.

The plot is almost perfectly symmetrical, centering around Gabriel Oak. He is a prosperous farmer at the beginning, he suffers financial reverses, and he emerges as an even more prosperous farmer at the end. He meets Bathsheba Everdene and falls in love with her, patiently supports her through her romantic adventures, and finally wins her. There is very little wasted material in the story; incidents that seem to have little importance earlier in the book loom significantly later on. For instance, as Fanny leaves Frank Troy in his barracks, laughter is heard "hardly distinguishable from the gurgle of the tiny whirlpools outside." The gurgle of these whirlpools is recalled by the deluging rain that carries off the flowers on Fanny's grave.

Although Hardy never ignored the public's reactions to his serialized novels and won his success in popular magazines, he remained a craftsman who never lost sight of his own ideal of the novel.

OUTSTANDING FEATURES

In Hardy's novels the characters that succeed, and are generally the happiest, are the ones that remain in harmony with their surroundings. The best example in this novel is, of course, Gabriel Oak. The most interesting characterization, however, is the almost collective use of the rustics. They manage to retain their individuality, but they seem to have a communal personality. They view the action of their social "betters" and comment on it, in a Greek-chorus-like effect. In addition, they help the action to progress. A good example of his occurs when Joseph Poorgrass is sent to bring Fanny's body back to Weatherbury. He lingers at the Buck's Head Inn so long that the body is brought to the churchyard too late for burial. Her body is then taken to Bathsheba at Weatherbury Farm for the night, and Bathsheba has time to open the coffin and discover Fanny's child.

The comedy associated with the rustics is almost Shakespearean. Hardy sympathizes with even the silliest characters (such as Poorgrass), and never laughs at them. Even Poorgrass can join in the merriment, as the tales of his timidity are presented. High spirits are again in evidence when Coggan coaxes Poorgrass to sing his "ballet" at the shearing feast.

Less important than Hardy's skill in depicting his rustic characters, but a distinct feature of his writing style, is his wide use of **allusion**. The unusual number of references, both classical and Biblical, is astonishing. The most effective **allusions** are the Biblical ones, since they seem to echo rugged strength of the pastoral setting. The choice of Bathsheba's name is an obvious device, but the use of Adam's first view of Eve as a comparison for Boldwood's awakening to Bathsheba's charms adds more substance to the **episode**. The comparison of Bathsheba to a nymph, or to Venus, is less subtle, and refines to Thor, Jove, Cyclops, etc., are often weak and ineffective, as well as incongruous.

Literary **allusions** are also included, such as Gabriel's bird's-eye view of Bathsheba "as Milton's Satan first saw Paradise," (from *Paradise Lost*), and the quotation from *Macbeth* to describe Gabriel's lack of skill in describing his feelings for Bathsheba.

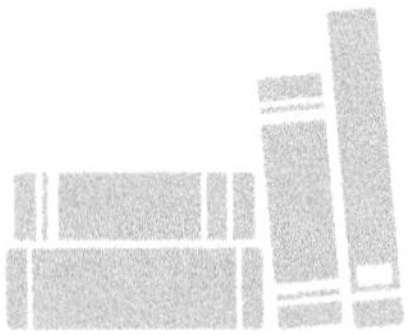

FAR FROM THE MADDING CROWD

SUMMARY

Gabriel Oak, a prosperous young farmer, meets a beautiful, though vain young lady (Bathsheba Everdene), whom he decides to marry. She refuses his proposal, however, since she does not love him, and is not yet ready to marry. He promises to love her always, but vows never to ask her to marry him again. Shortly after, her uncle dies, and she inherits his farm at Weatherbury. She leaves Norcombe, and Gabriel, already disappointed in love and unaware of Bathsheba's new position in life, suffers a grave financial loss when his sheep fall into a chalk pit. He is forced to sell everything he owns to pay his debts.

Since he is unsuccessful in finding a place as bailiff or as shepherd, Gabriel makes his way toward Weatherbury. He helps to put out a fire in a hayrick and hopes to get a place as shepherd on this farm. He is surprised to find that Bathsheba owns the farm. She hires him as shepherd and he goes to the local malthouse to inquire about lodgings. At the malthouse he is welcomed by the villagers; as the group begins to leave, news is brought of the dismissal of Bathsheba's bailiff for stealing, and of the sudden disappearance of Fanny Robin, the youngest of the maidservants at Weatherbury Farm.

Bathsheba decides to manage the farm herself and goes to Casterbridge to the grain market. She is annoyed when she is ignored by one of the farmers, Mr. Boldwood. He has led a solitary existence on the next farm, and he has a reputation for being a confirmed bachelor. On a wild impulse, she sends him an anonymous valentine, inscribed "Marry me." From Gabriel, Boldwood learns that the handwriting is Bathsheba's, and his interest in her is aroused. He falls in love with her, and one day, as she and her laborers are involved in washing her sheep, he approaches and asks her to marry him.

She refuses this offer, and when he begs her again and again to accept, she asks for more time. She seeks out Gabriel as he is grinding shears and asks his opinion. Gabriel is still deeply in love with her, but answers her honestly; he strongly disapproves of her conduct. She is angered by his reply and tells him to leave the farm. Gabriel agrees to leave immediately. The very next day her sheep are injured, and she is forced to send for Gabriel. He ignores her first request and then comes to save the sheep, when she pleads with him not to desert her.

Meanwhile, Fanny Robin is reported to have run away with Francis Troy, an army sergeant. She follows him to his new post and anxiously inquires about their marriage. He seems hesitant about his plans, but promises to meet her as soon as he can.

At Weatherbury Farm the rustics gather to help shear the sheep. After the shearing, a gay feast takes place, and Boldwood appears to act as host. He again asks Bathsheba to marry him and is sorry for her foolish valentine.. When she reveals about five or six weeks.

That night, however, she accidentally meets Troy and is charmed by his manner and his good looks. She meets him again during the hay gathering and is secretly pleased by his compliments. She is further impressed by his daring swordplay; she refuses to see how unstable a character he is, and that he has little beyond his charm to offer. Gabriel tries to warm her about Troy; though he still loves her, he advises her that marrying Boldwood would be safer than marrying Troy. She meets Boldwood and firmly refuses to marry him, although she pities him and is sorry for her foolish Valentine. When she reveals that she loves Troy, Boldwood speaks out violently against him. Bathsheba follows Troy to Bath to warm him about Boldwood; when Troy hints about another beauty who is interested in him, she marries him to be certain of keeping him.

Troy returns with her to Weatherbury, and Boldwood offers him money first to marry Fanny, and then to marry Bathsheba. Troy shows him the newspaper report of his marriage to Bathsheba and throws the money into the road. Boldwood swears he will punish him some day. Gabriel's disappointment and sorrow at this rash marriage increases as he watches the effect of the news on Boldwood. He allows his farm to deteriorate and seems to have lost his stability.

Troy celebrates his new prosperity at a harvest supper and dance. Gabriel notices signs of a threatening storm which could ruin Bathsheba's harvest, but Troy ignores his warnings and insists that the farm workers join him in an all-night drinking party. Gabriel, with Bathsheba's help, manages to cover the gathered sheaves and save the crop.

Fanny Robin again appears in the story, painfully making her way to a poorhouse in Casterbridge. She uses her last bit of strength to reach the door and is carried inside, evidently very ill.

Bathsheba has become suspicious of her husband's interest in Fanny and guesses how strong the attachment had been. He receives word from Fanny to meet her at Casterbridge, and he rides there the same day that news of her death reaches Bathsheba. In charity, Bathsheba sends Poorgrass for the body and arranges to have it buried in the churchyard. He delays at the Buck's Head Inn and arrives too late for the burial. Fanny's body is taken to her last known home-Weatherbury Farm-for the night, and Bathsheba cannot resist opening the coffin. She discovers the secret that Gabriel had hoped to keep from her; buried with Fanny is her child that died at birth. Troy returns at this point and insists that Fanny meant more to him than anyone else could. He arranges to have an elaborate monument placed on her grave and he personally arranges flowers, which are washed away in the evening's rain. Troy leaves Weatherbury and apparently drowns, although his body is never found.

Boldwood again begs Bathsheba to marry him and she finally agrees although she insists on a waiting period of seven years, when Troy would be legally dead, or some trace of his body might be found. Boldwood prepares a Christmas party, during which the engagement would be announced. A surprise guest arrives and reveals himself as Troy. He orders Bathsheba to return to the farm with him, and, as she shrinks back from him, Boldwood shoots him.

Boldwood is convicted of murder, but his death sentence is commuted to imprisonment when the villagers plead for his life. Troy is buried with Fanny; Bathsheba slowly regains her health and her composure. Gabriel decides to leave Weatherbury and England and tells Bathsheba of his plans. She suddenly realizes how dependent she is upon him and how much his love means to her. Her own feeling for him is not the reckless passion she felt for Troy, but a quiet respect for his fine character. Remembering that Gabriel had promised not to ask her again, she goes to his cottage and asks him to stay as her husband. He agrees that her request is as it should be; the two marry and enjoy a life of quiet serenity.

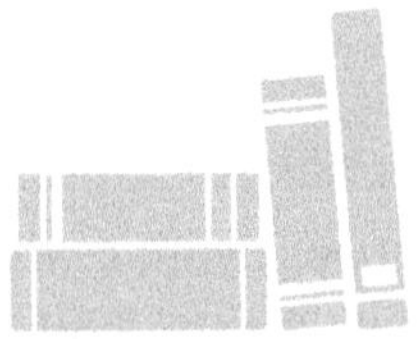

FAR FROM THE MADDING CROWD

TEXTUAL ANALYSIS

CHAPTERS 1-10

CHAPTER I: DESCRIPTION OF FARMER OAK - AN INCIDENT

Gabriel Oak is introduced in rather neutral tones; he is far from the dashing hero of many novels, and seems to be a solid young man of the community, neither overly-impressive nor unrespected. His outward appearance is proper and staid, rather than charming or fascinating, and his neighbors know him for his good character and judgment. He is far from being insipid or colorless, however; even though he is simple and straightforward, he is not a weak man. He has an air of dignity and self-confidence, and shows a quiet assurance and maturity beyond his twenty-eight years. Although established on his own little sheep farm, he is still a bachelor.

As he was in a field one morning, he spots a wagon making its way down the highway, through a spur of Norcombe Hill. The wagon is colorfully painted and loaded with household goods. Perched on top of the wagon is a very pretty young woman, wearing a bright red jacket. As Gabriel watches, the wagon stops, and the wagoner announces that the tail board has fallen off, and that he will run back to get it.

The young lady takes advantage of the pause to untie one of the wrapped parcels near her. Once she has satisfied herself that no one is in sight, she unwraps the enclosed mirror and spends some minutes in examining herself attentively and with evident approval. Gabriel realizes that she is vain; there is no practical need for her to use the mirror, she merely enjoys looking at her reflection, perhaps dreaming of herself as a popular beauty.

As the wagoner returns, she slips the mirror back into its wrappings and the journey is resumed. Gabriel follows the wagon at a short distance and sees it stopped at the toll gate. The young lady refuses to pay the extra two pence that the gate keeper demands, and Gabriel resolves the stalemate by paying the extra fee for her. She seems indifferent to his kindness, not even feeling the need for an expression of gratitude, and even seems annoyed that she lost her point of dispute. The wagon goes on and Gabriel discusses the young lady with the gate keeper. The keeper finds her beautiful indeed, but Gabriel points out that she has obvious faults. The keeper suggests "pride," and Gabriel sadly adds "vanity."

Comment

The novel begins, and will end, with Gabriel. He serves as a kind of touchstone by which we may measure the characters and events of the novel. The opening description hints of his reliability in this respect; he is a self-effacing young man and yet observant and interested in happenings about him. His concern for other characters is evidenced by his remote, but interested, study of the young lady, and by his offering to pay the trivial fee she owes. His shrewd perception and unromantic nature also makes the reader implicitly trust him as the point-of-perspective.

CHAPTER II: NIGHT - THE FLOCK - AN INTERIOR - ANOTHER INTERIOR

A beautiful description of a clear, cold winter's night on Norcombe Hill, and its effect on an observer, opens the chapter. A solitary visitor would be struck not only with the starkness of the chalk and soil covered ridge, but by the sounds and the sensation of motion, not only of the trees and grass, but of the earth itself. The skies seem more brilliantly colored, and like the stars brighter and especially close. Suddenly, a sound different from those of nature's can be heard: Gabriel's flute.

The notes are a bit muffled, since Gabriel is playing inside his little sheep hut. This special hut resembles a toy Noah's Ark; it is mobile and serves the shepherd as a temporary shelter, when the lambing season demands his special attention.

Gabriel is especially concerned with the birth of the lambs, since he has only recently acquired the stock and land, and the status of independent farmer. His entire investment is bound up in the raising of sheep, so proper care both of the sheep and the new lambs is essential to his success, and the sheep must be supervised personally. Gabriel stops playing and leaves to inspect his flock. He returns with a newly-born lamb that needs some special care. He places the lamb near the small fire and quickly falls asleep.

The interior of the hut is comfortable, but simple; instead of windows, two round holes with wooden slides serve to let in air. In addition to Gabriel's flute and some food, the hut contains whatever equipment he might need to care for his sheep. When the lamb, now warmed by the fire, begins to bleat, Gabriel awakes, instantly alert. He leaves the hut to return the lamb to the flock, and searches the sky for signs to guess the time of night. Even after he realizes that it is about one o'clock, he remains charmed by the beauty of the view. He sees a light that he at first mistakes for another star and walks toward it. He finds a little shed built on the slope of the hill, and from the roof (which is nearly level with the ground, at that point), he sees two cows being tended by a middle-aged woman and a younger woman, who is wrapped in a long cloak. One cow has just given birth to a calf, and the other has been given bran-mash treatments. The older woman remarks that she is relieved that the cow is better, even though her rest has been broken in caring for it. The younger woman seems indifferent to the cow's fate; she wishes that they could hire a man to take care of their stock, and adds that the wind has carried off her hat. Since the bran supply has given out, the younger woman plans to ride to the mill early in the morning, even though the other woman reminds her that they have no side-saddle.

Gabriel becomes curious about the young woman; he wishes he could see her face, and imagines her to be a beauty. At this point, the girl drops her cloak and Gabriel recognizes her as the young lady who stared at herself; in the mirror, as she sat on top of the wagon. After placing the calf near its mother, the two women take the lantern and leave. Gabriel returns to his flock.

Comment

There is little action in the first two chapters, as Hardy establishes both his rustic setting and his means of evaluating character and action: the "natural" world of rural England. In this peaceful pastoral setting (with especial focus on sheep raising), far from the busy city life, characters are given a chance to lead happy lives, if they will only remain true to their closeness with nature. Gabriel's connection with the world of nature is shown from the first sentence of the novel, in which he is compared to the rising sun. His last name suggests the oak's permanence and stability. His world is definitely unmechanical; although he keeps the family watch oh his person, it is not always accurate, and he relies on his neighbors' timepieces, or the position of the stars, or the length of shadows to tell him the time. He seems more "at home" out-of-doors, and well-suited to the life of a farmer.

The young lady he watches is quite different. She acts unnaturally; she shows her pride and vanity by viewing herself in the mirror, and doesn't even consider the need to thank Gabriel for paying her extra toll. She is indifferent to the care of the cows, while Gabriel carefully tends his lambs himself. His happiness and eventual success is promised by his basic honesty of character and his closeness with the world of nature. The young lady, on the other hand, seems destined for unhappiness and suffering, since she is so proud and so distant from the "real" world.

CHAPTER III: A GIRL ON HORSEBACK - CONVERSATION

At daybreak on the next day, Oak goes to a grove of beech trees and finds the young lady's hat in a ditch. He takes it back to his hut and awaits the arrival of the young lady, who is riding towards him. She looks to see if anyone is around, and then lies flat backward on her pony, as she passes under the level boughs of the trees surrounding the path. She rides on to Tewnell Mill, and Oak, amused and a bit surprised at her acrobatic feat, hangs up her hat in the hut and goes out to his flock. On her return, she takes the milk pail to the cow shed and Gabriel waits on the path to return her hat. She is startled by his sudden appearance from behind the hedge, and he is able to see her more clearly. Her beauty is set off by the modesty of a rural maid; she is poised and composed as Gabriel stares at her, and it is he who blushes. She claims her hat and tells him she knows who he is. When he tells her that he had seen her on the way to the mill, she realizes that he had seen her antics, and she blushes, but Gabriel is even more embarrassed than she. He tactfully turns his head to give her a chance to regain her poise, but when he turns around again, she has gone.

For five days after this meeting, she comes regularly to the shed to milk the cows. She doesn't look for Gabriel and seems to be annoyed at his lack of tact. Gabriel regrets acknowledging his invasion of her privacy. He has been watching the shed on a particularly cold afternoon, and when he returns to his little hut, he leaves the ventilating holes shut, in order to warm the hut quickly. He ignores the possible danger of suffocation and falls asleep. He awakes to find the young lady trying to revive him; he blames the hut for being unsafe, but she reminds him that he was wrong in leaving the holes closed. She tells him that his dog led her there; he is grateful to her for saving his life and thanks her. She teases him by not giving him her name, and then leaves.

Comment

The sense of freedom and love of independence that the young lady enjoys is exemplified by her ride to the mill. Her acrobatic feat is "tomboyish," but also an indication of her disregard of conventional behavior, as well as her youthful pleasure in just being able to ride through such a lovely scene.

The young lady had never found it necessary to thank Gabriel for helping her at the toll gate, or for finding her hat for her, but she repays this debt many times over by her rescue of Gabriel from death. She, unfortunately, dispels the quiet mood in the hut by her insistence on teasing Gabriel about holding her hand and about discovering her name.

CHAPTER IV: GABRIEL'S RESOLVE - THE VISIT - THE MISTAKE

Gabriel's interest in the young lady grows quietly but surely; he finds out that she is Bathsheba Everdene, and that she is staying with her aunt at a cottage nearby. He likes to repeat her name again and again; he watches for her without being able to put his feelings for her into exact words. She is totally unaware of his feelings; he spends hours thinking about her, and then decides to ask her to marry him. He dreads the day when the cow's milk would dry up and she would not return to the cow shed. When several days have passed without her coming, he tries to think of an errand to take him to her aunt's home.

When one of his ewes dies, he takes the opportunity of offering Bathsheba the orphaned lamb for a pet. Dressed carefully and tastefully, he sets out on a fine day. As he approaches, his dog chases the household cat behind some bushes, and Gabriel hears a woman's voice comforting the cat. He defends his dog, but receives no answer. He wonders if the voice was Bathsheba's and how his proposal would be affected by this unlucky accident.

He is a bit embarrassed as he meets Bathsheba's aunt; she tells him Bathsheba is out, and he asks her to tell Bathsheba only that "Someone" has called. He tells the aunt that he plans to propose to Bathsheba and questions her about Bathsheba's suitors. She indicates that several young men are interested in her niece. Gabriel privately regrets his own "ordinariness," but feels that there is some hope for him, since he is the first to propose. He decides not to wait for Bathsheba, and starts to return home, but Bathsheba races after him. She tells him that her aunt made a mistake in sending him away from courting her, and in allowing him to think she had many suitors. The delighted Gabriel thinks that she is encouraging him, and tries to take her hand, but she slips it behind her. He promises her to work twice as hard on his farm, and to do anything to make her happy. But Gabriel had misunderstood her following him. She had only wanted him not to have the idea that she was so admired; if she really had wanted him to propose, she tells him, she would not have run after him. He asks her again to marry him, and she, confused by the openness of the world out-of-doors, is momentarily distracted. He offers to make her life a happy one; she may have a piano (he will play his flute to her accompaniment), a gig, flowers and birds (poultry). He will even publish the marriage (and any subsequent births) in the local newspaper. Although she would enjoy being a bride, the prospect of married life, especially with a husband she does not love, does not appeal to her.

She is not heartless, and tells him that she is sorry she can't marry him, even though he loves her so much. She is sorry now that she followed him, and tries to comfort him by telling him that she is better educated than he, and that he would be better off marrying a rich wife, since he is still a young farmer. He agrees that a rich wife would be a more practical choice for him, but it is she that he loves. When he again presses his offer, she refuses, and he promises that, though he will love and want her until he dies, he will never ask her to marry him again.

Comment

One of Bathsheba's main faults is revealed in this **episode**. She is selfish enough to want to be liked and admired without sacrificing anything herself. She refuses to be seriously committed to anyone; her impulsive following of Gabriel indicates that she will act on serious matters, without reflecting on the outcome of her actions.

Hardy makes use of **irony** in presenting Gabriel's promise. It is only at the end of the book, however, when Bathsheba remembers that promise and must act herself because of it, that the full impact of the promise is revealed. She is humbled because of it and becomes a happier woman.

CHAPTER V: DEPARTURE OF BATHSHEBA - A PASTORAL TRAGEDY

At this point, Gabriel's fortunes really come to a low point. He discovers that Bathsheba has left her aunt's farm, and he doesn't know where she has gone. Her abrupt departure is more emphatic than her verbal refusal of his offer. It is hard for him to fall out of love; the flame still lingers after her departure, but her absence does not cause him to over-idealize her. His brief acquaintance with Bathsheba's aunt makes it difficult for him to get news about her; indirectly, he learns that she has gone to Weatherbury (about twenty miles away), but cannot find out if her stay there will be permanent.

In addition, **catastrophe** strikes him on his farm, through the inexperience of one of his dogs. His old sheep dog, George, is past his prime, and Gabriel hopes to replace him with one of his own puppies. The young dog thinks he is doing his job by keeping the sheep on the run; one night, the force of the running sheep causes the flock to break through a safety rail above a chalk pit. Gabriel is awakened by the violent ringing of the sheep bells and hurries out to discover that about two hundred ewes, with their unborn lambs, are dead or dying at the foot of the pit. He had bought and stocked the farm with a credit-like arrangement; his entire investment has been lost. His first thought is to pity the dead animals and especially the lambs that never had a chance to live. He is relieved that he hadn't married Bathsheba before this terrible calamity struck. Oak sells the rest of his stock, his tools, and his land to pay his debts; he is left with little more than his clothes.

Comment

Gabriel's double loss is accepted with resignation and perseverance. His reaction to his troubles gives the reader a good glimpse of the nobility of his character. In addition, the depth of Gabriel's relationship with nature is shown in his first reaction to the sight of the dead sheep, that is, pity for them. He doesn't think of his financial loss until he has mourned their sad end, and felt relief that Bathsheba has been spared this reversal. His total lack of selfishness is a fine foil to Bathsheba's preoccupation with herself, as revealed in the last chapter.

CHAPTER VI: THE FAIR - THE JOURNEY - THE FIRE

Two months later, Gabriel is discovered at the hiring fair in Casterbridge. About two or three hundred men wearing some special sign to show their specialties (for instance, shepherds carry crooks) are waiting to hire themselves out as carters, wagoners, thatchers, shepherds, etc. Gabriel, still dignified despite his hard blow, is trying to find a place as bailiff, but shepherds seem to be in demand. After he buys a crook from a smith and exchanges his overcoat for a shepherd's smock, it seems that now bailiffs are in demand. Two or three interested farmers turn away when they learn that Gabriel had once been a sheep farmer himself. By late afternoon, Gabriel has still not been hired, but plays his flute gaily, rather than give in to despair. He earns a few pennies by his playing and learns that another fair will be held at Shottsford, ten miles beyond Weatherbury (five or six miles away). Since Weatherbury people were known to be pleasant and interesting, Gabriel decides to sleep at Weatherbury on his way to Shottsford.

He walks along for three or four miles, until it begins to get very dark. When he finds a wagon on the side of the road, apparently deserted, he decides to sleep in the wagon and save lodging money. After a meal of bread, ham and some cider, he falls asleep in the hay piled in the wagon; he wakes to find the wagon moving. It is now about nine o'clock (according to the stars); Gabriel listens to the two men in the front of the wagon (Billy Smallbury and Joseph Poorgrass), as they discuss a proud young woman who is mistress of the farm on which they work. Gabriel wonders if this could be Bathsheba, but decides that it is only a wild guess. He slips off the wagon, deciding to sleep in a field, rather than walk into town. He sees an unusually bright light about a half mile away, and realizes there must be a fire. He makes his way across a field towards the fire and finds a straw stack burning. The stack is nearly destroyed, but a wheat rick, as well as a whole series of stacks, is dangerously near. Then men who have come to fight the fire are hopelessly confused; Gabriel hurries over to supervise as best he can. He organizes the workers and personally does much of the work to put out the blaze; a young woman watches him, beyond the light of the fire. She asks who the shepherd is, and sends words to thank him. Gabriel hopes to ask for a job as shepherd, and questions the workers about the owner of the farm. He learns that the farm belongs to a young lady who inherited it after the death of her uncle. Although he is wet and dirty from fighting the fire, Gabriel hurries over to the young lady whom the laborers have pointed out. He asks if she needs a shepherd, and, as she lifts her face veil, he sees Bathsheba again. Humbly, he repeats his request.

Comment

In at least two places in the novel, Hardy makes use of a popular device for suspense in hiding Bathsheba's identity. Wilkie Collins (author of *The Moonstone, The Woman in White*), had made the device famous, and when he began his career as novelist, these novels were pointed out to Hardy as good examples to follow.

Gabriel's strength of character in being able to persevere, despite his disappointments and setbacks, is captured in his playing the flute at the hiring fair. His playing is quickly rewarded by some pennies that he desperately needs, but it also will make him a welcome newcomer to the Weatherbury community.

CHAPTER VII: RECOGNITION - A TIMID GIRL

This meeting is awkward for both of them; Bathsheba feels some pity, as well as pride, at the change in their circumstances. She does need a shepherd, and the rustic laborers agree that he is a perfect choice. She sends Gabriel to her bailiff and promises to send some refreshments for her workers to Warren's Malthouse. When Gabriel asks the bailiff about lodgings, he is told to go to the malthouse, and someone there can help him. As he walks toward the malthouse, Gabriel thinks about this surprising meeting and of Bathsheba's new status. As he reaches the churchyard, he meets a poorly-dressed girl, and asks her the way to the malthouse. He senses that the girl is troubled in some way, but she only asks him how late Buck's Head Inn is open, and refuses any offer of help. Since Gabriel is strange to the neighborhood, he cannot tell her; she asks him not to reveal, until a few days had passed, that he had seen her. When she shivers in the cold, Gabriel charitably gives her his one spare shilling, and then walks on towards Weatherbury. He knows that the girl is troubled and sad-her pulse beats like the trembling of a frightened lamb - but he can do nothing else for her.

Comment

Again Hardy keeps the identity of the woman Gabriel meets on the way to the malthouse a source of suspense and curiosity. This "veiled woman" is not identified until the end of the next chapter.

Gabriel's instinctive generosity is viewed in his sharing (literally) his last shilling with her. He realizes that she is in trouble, and would like to help her, but she is shy of confidences and he is a stranger in the village and cannot guess at her difficulty. The incident has further use in the novel; since Gabriel has been so kind to her, the young lady writes to thank him, and lets slip some information about her present condition.

CHAPTER VIII: THE MALTHOUSE - THE CHAT - THE NEWS

The malthouse is a thatched, ivy-colored building, with a stone-flag floor, a large kiln (oven), in the center, and a settle, or bench, for the malt drinkers' comfort, on the side of the room. The old malster had seen several generations pass; when Gabriel enters and is greeted by the men, the malster tells him that he knew Gabriel's family and several people at Norcombe. He orders a clean mug for Gabriel, but Gabriel insists that the mug, dusty from the ashes of the fire, is good enough for him, and is immediately accepted by the rustics as a welcome addition to the group. The members of the group of rustics are identified: Henry Fray, who insists his name is "Henery," merry Jan Coggan, congenial Mark Clark, Jacob Smallbury, the malster's son, and bashful Joseph Poorgrass.

After the rustics tell some amusing stories about Poorgrass's timidity, a brief silence follows, broken by Gabriel's questions about the farm and its new owner. He finds it hard to keep the villagers from rambling on about Farmer Everdene and his family, and from telling stories about the village past. He finds out very little about Bathsheba's past (she was not too pretty as a child), and the villagers hint that most of the business of the farm is carried on by the bailiff, and that he is not too honest. Gabriel changes the subject and talks about the malster's age. With little encouragement, he gives his past history and judges that he must be over a hundred years old.

As the mug of malt is passed around, Gabriel's flute is noticed and Henery recognizes Gabriel as the man who played the flute at the fair. Gabriel confesses his need of money, but the villagers still welcome him, despite his poverty. They request a tune, and Gabriel plays until he is complimented by Laban Tall (a man with so little individuality that he is constantly referred to as "Susan Tall's husband"). The villagers recognize Gabriel as a clever man and are delighted to have him join their group. Tall starts to leave the malthouse, and the group begins to break up for the evening. Henery hurries in with news that the bailiff has been dismissed for stealing; Bathsheba caught him with a half bushel of barley and had discovered that at least five sacks had been stolen. If he leaves immediately, she promises not to prosecute him. Tall returns with more news; Fanny Robin, the youngest of the maidservants at Weatherbury Farm, is missing; the possibility of suicide is suggested, and some hints about her running away with a soldier are made. The rustics hurry back to the farm to start the search for Fanny, as Gabriel reflects on the events of the evening and decides to get his belongings from Norcombe.

Comment

This chapter is wonderful for its comedy. The anecdotes and stories are amusing themselves, and the humor increases as the malster, or another rustic, rambles on and on, as Gabriel patiently waits for news of Bathsheba.

Hardy sketches the individuals in some detail (too long to be included here), and the reader is left with a distinct impression of each man. The novelist often accomplishes this by identifying a particular trait with a man (such as Poorgrass's timidity, or Coggan's sharing of the drinking cup). Yet, the group is so carefully united (especially by their common tie with the past) that each member acts in harmony with the others.

The fact that the chapters were presented serially is evident by the tantalizing or "teasing" ending. In this chapter, we receive the sensational news of Fanny's disappearance; Victorian readers were sure to want to see Cornhill's next issue to find out more about it, and to see if Gabriel would replace Bathsheba's bailiff.

CHAPTER IX: THE HOMESTEAD - A VISITOR - HALF-CONFIDENCES

Weatherbury Farm is described as a Classic Renaissance building, with later additions in different architectural styles. It had apparently once been a manor hall in the center of the estate; its age is evident from the moss which covers its walls. The front of the house is formal and seems little-used; it is the back door which is used for most of the business on the farm.

Bathsheba and Liddy are sorting papers and various articles left by Bathsheba's uncle, when a gentleman appears at the front door. He announces himself as Mr. Boldwood, a neighboring farmer, but Bathsheba sends down word to say that she is not at home. She feels too dust-covered and preoccupied to see him. He has come to inquire if there is any news of Fanny Robin. Bathsheba questions Liddy (who has become more of a companion and confidant than maid since Bathsheba's arrival) about him. Liddy reports that he had sent Fanny to school and had helped her to get her place at the farm. He is described as a confirmed bachelor. The little Coggan boy tells them that Boldwood gave him a penny for opening the gate, and that Boldwood had asked about Bathsheba. Bathsheba teases one of the servants about not being married, and when Liddy asks if Bathsheba has ever had a proposal, she hints mysteriously about Gabriel and says that the young man had not been quite good enough for her. Their conversation is interrupted by the arrival of the laborers.

Comment

Hardy's architectural background is noted in his description of the farm house, and the use of such terms as: "finials" (crowning ornamental architectural detail) and "vermiculations" (worm eaten).

From Boldwood's first attempt to meet Bathsheba, his progress is marked by misunderstanding and unfortunate circumstances. Had Bathsheba been prepared to welcome her neighbor, her curiosity about him would have been quickly satisfied. Had Boldwood met Bathsheba, her impression upon him might have been less devastating. His sensible reserved nature might have rejected her youthful impetuosity and her remoteness, made romantic by her remaining a stranger, would have been less emphatic.

Bathsheba's rejection of Gabriel as a suitor marks her as a proud, selfish young lady. She had never really investigated his qualities; he is dismissed as a possible husband only because she feels that he is not her social equal.

CHAPTER X: MISTRESS AND MEN

About a half-hour later, Bathsheba officiates as mistress of the farm and pays her laborers for their time and goods. She announces that the bailiff has been dismissed and that she will manage the farm on her own. Reports about Fanny are presented; the Newmill Pond has been dragged; one of the men has been sent to Casterbridge to look for her (Gabriel has quietly inquired for Fanny at the Buck's Heads Inn). With his constant advice, Henery tries to take over the farm management, but Bathsheba firmly refuses his help. Since Gabriel needs an assistant, Cain Bell (mistakenly so named instead of "Abel") is proposed and accepted. Bathsheba speaks to Gabriel very coolly, insisting on establishing her new position. Billy Smallbury returns from Casterbridge and suggests that Fanny had left with one of the soldiers of the Eleventh Dragoon Guards. The name of the young man is not revealed, but he is supposed to be a sergeant. Bathsheba sends word of this conclusion to Boldwood and addresses the group about her new authority. She leaves the room with the pride and dignity of a queen; Liddy trails in her wake in unconscious **parody** of her mistress.

Comment

Bathsheba has reached the peak of her happiness; she is admired and respected in her new position of authority. Her pride and vanity are gently mocked by Hardy as he describes Liddy's assuming the airs and sense of importance that are so vital to her mistress.

FAR FROM THE MADDING CROWD

TEXTUAL ANALYSIS

CHAPTERS 11-20

CHAPTER XI: OUTSIDE THE BARRACKS - SNOW - A MEETING

On a dark, snowy night, a small figure approaches the army barracks in a small town north of Weatherbury. The scene is bare and desolate; the only sound is the muffled striking of the bell. The figure is that of a young woman; she tosses snow balls (not very expertly) at one of the windows. She finally succeeds in striking the right window and gets the attention of someone inside. She asks for Sergeant Troy, and the man admits that he is the sergeant himself. She tells him that she is Fanny Robin; he is surprised that she has followed him such a distance. When she asks if he has arranged for her marriage, he presents several difficulties (she needs clothes, a special license must be obtained, he must get an officer's permission, etc.). She is disappointed to discover that he has forgotten to get the permission before, but he explains that her arrival here was totally unexpected. She asks him to meet her at Mrs. Twill's rooming house. As she leaves, a sound of laughter can be heard, but since it was not very clear she may have missed it.

Comment

It is interesting to notice that Fanny is always pictured alone; she seems to have no friends except Troy, and in the few **episodes** in which she appears she is either travelling to find him, or waiting to meet him. An extra note of sympathy is constantly struck for her, in her companionless existence.

CHAPTER XII: FARMERS - A RULE - AN EXCEPTION

On the next market day, Bathsheba makes her first appearance in her new role as farm-manager, at the public cornmarket in Casterbridge. She is the only woman at the market, and feels a bit nervous about the impression she will make and the reception she will receive. She decides that she must be practical to succeed as a buyer and seller, and she begins to speak with confidence and poise. She retains her femininity despite her practical manner, and she is welcomed as a nice contrast to the rougher male group. Only one man seems immune to her charm; he is a mature gentleman, characterized by his dignity, and Bathsheba guesses that he is unmarried. After the fair, she returns home with Liddy and asks about this unusual man. She is annoyed at Liddy's lack of information, but, when the man passes them on the road Liddy recognizes him as Mr. Boldwood. Gossip about him reports that he has been unhappy in love, and Bathsheba prefers this romantic version to explain his long bachelorhood to the more realistic explanation that Boldwood has just never paid any attention to women before, and is a controlled and reserved man by nature.

Comment

Bathsheba's constant wish to be admired and respected finds its fulfillment at the market; she is the center of attention (as the only woman) and is grateful for the reception she receives. She is not satisfied by this general acceptance, however, and resents the indifference of the farmer (who eventually is identified as Boldwood).

His cool reserve annoys her; had she only welcomed him when he called at her house, this indifference might have been changed. As it is, Boldwood has a mysterious, remote air that Bathsheba girlishly translates as resulting from an unhappy love affair.

CHAPTER XIII: SORTES SANCTORUM - THE VALENTINE

On the thirteenth of February, Bathsheba and Liddy are sitting together chatting, and Liddy suggests that Bathsheba use the Bible and key to guess at her future husband. This seems to be an old custom, and the rust marks on one of the pages of the Book of Ruth suggest that the Bible has been used for this purpose many times before. Bathsheba turns the book, but does not identify any young man that might be indicated. Liddy has noticed that Boldwood seems to be in Bathsheba's thoughts, and, as Bathsheba writes out a valentine for little Teddy Coggan, she suggests that Bathsheba send the letter to Boldwood instead. The gesture seems to be so opposed to common sense, that Bathsheba tosses a hymn book (to see if it would fall open or shut) to help her make her decision about sending it. The book falls down shut, and Bathsheba directs the envelope to Boldwood, sealing it with the words, "Marry me." She then sends off the valentine.

Comment

However headstrong or wild her actions had been in the past, Bathsheba had never been made to suffer for them. At best, the valentine is a crude joke; but the apex of her success has been reached, and the tide of circumstance, and retribution, is beginning to turn against her. Her earlier actions had involved only herself; now that she is toying with another's feelings just for her own amusement, she must in turn be made to suffer.

CHAPTER XIV: EFFECT OF THE LETTER - SUNRISE

Boldwood seems fascinated by the valentine; he stares at it so intensely that he seems to be asking it what its significance might be. Until dusk, he keeps the valentine on the mantel; when he prepares for bed, he places it in the corner of the mirror in his room. He is always conscious of it; its arrival has unleashed a flood of feelings. He endlessly speculates on the sender and tries to guess why it was sent. His sleep is haunted by these endless questionings. The dawn freshness of the outdoor world seems particularly in evidence at daybreak, but Boldwood is still concerned with the mysterious valentine, and hardly notices anything around him.

The mailcart appears and he is given a letter, but it is meant for Gabriel. He sees Gabriel walking in the distance and volunteers to bring the letter to him. Gabriel is on his way to the malthouse, and Boldwood follows him there.

Comment

Never has Boldwood's poise and reserve been so disturbed; the motions long controlled and almost forgotten begin to stir. Boldwood has had little interest in women before, and not because they did not express an interest in him. The little mystery surrounding the valentine adds another dimension to this situation; he is curious about the sender.

The slow chipping away at his character and mental equilibrium begins; gradually, he must change his temperament and manner. It is ironic that he is the one man who would take such a valentine so seriously, and become so affected by it.

CHAPTER XV: A MORNING MEETING - THE LETTER AGAIN

The malster is at his breakfast of bread and bacon, when he is joined by Henery, Moon, Poorgrass and other carters and wagoners. Bathsheba's management of the farm without a bailiff becomes the topic of discussion. Henery feels that leaving Bathsheba in charge can only lead to disaster, but his statement is colored by his own disappointment in not being made bailiff. Her pride and vanity are also criticized, but her cleverness and her evident good education seem to be saving graces for her. After a pause, Bathsheba's piano and her change of her uncle's furniture for more elaborate chairs and tables are commented upon. Gabriel, radiating health and vigor, enters carrying four newly-born lambs. He and Cainy have been busy all night, caring for the ewes and the new lambs. Since he has no lambing hut, he asks if the lambs could be placed by the fire in order to warm and strengthen them. The malster first reminisces about Norcombe, and then the conversation turns back to Bathsheba. Gabriel threatens anyone who would speak out against her with the power of his fist.

Gabriel's qualifications are examined and admired; everyone agrees that he would be the perfect choice for bailiff because of his cleverness, his accomplishments (especially in being able to tell time by the stars), and for his farming skill. He agrees that he would like to be bailiff, and thinks he would make a good one, but he supports Bathsheba's right to manage the farm in her own way, and he rejects the idea that he is being poorly treated.

Boldwood enters and gives Gabriel the letter from Fanny Robin. She thanks him for his help and tells him that she is going to marry Frank Troy. Troy's history is revealed by Boldwood; he is illegitimately descended from nobility. He has had a good education, and worked as a lawyer's clerk in Casterbridge, but he enlisted as a soldier, and seemed to have ruined any good prospects he might have had.

Cainy Bell brings Gabriel news that two more ewes have had twin lambs; before Gabriel returns to the flock, he marks the lambs he has brought to the malthouse with Bathsheba's initials. Boldwood hesitantly follows Gabriel, and, finally gathering enough strength to make the request, asks Gabriel if he knows whose handwriting is on the anonymous valentine. Gabriel identifies it as Bathsheba's, and he realizes that the letter must have been sent anonymously for Boldwood to ask. Boldwood tries to pass off his questions lightly, but any suggestion of humor would be lost by a glance at his tortured face. Regretting his revealing of his private affairs to a stranger, he returns to his house to set the valentine on the mantel again, and to reflect on the news of its sender.

Comment

Boldwood's slow movement away from his former character is evidenced in his questioning Gabriel about the valentine. He would hardly have allowed his private affairs to be even hinted to a casual stranger, but the impact of this valentine has set feelings and reactions into motion that cannot be retracted.

Fanny's letter follows Gabriel's kindness to her. It allows the plot to develop enough for the reader to realize that Fanny's elopement may be a fact, but not her marriage. Hardy rarely wastes incidents in his novels; this **episode** is a good example of one action causing another.

CHAPTER XVI: ALL SAINTS' AND ALL SOULS'

At the end of the weekday service, the congregation at All Saints' Church is startled to see a young soldier in his red uniform striding up the aisle. The curiosity he excites causes them to delay their departure and await the outcome of this unusual visit. The curate and the soldier converse briefly, and then the clerk and his wife are called to the chancel steps.

The rumor quickly spreads that a wedding is about to take place. The clock strikes half past eleven, and the young lady has not yet appeared. The soldier grows more visibly embarrassed as the moments pass; he stands rigidly at attention, never moving.

The long delay causes more whispers and giggling, and then, by the time the noon hour is struck, there is dead silence. The curate and the clerk leave the chancel; the soldier finally turns to face the curious crowd, then strides firmly out of the church.

As he crosses the paved square opposite the church, he meets a young woman, obviously distressed and terror-stricken when she greets him. She has gone to All Souls' Church by mistake and had waited there for him. She asks if the wedding can take place on the next day, but he has been so embarrassed and annoyed by her mistake, that he tells her he will not go through such an experience again for a long while. When she begs him to forgive her and to tell her when they can be married, he only mutters, "God knows."

Comment

Troy speaks the words "God knows" in light **irony**, but the tragic impact of his careless statement strikes him later in the novel. It is to Troy's credit that he arranges for the wedding; from Boldwood's description of him, it is a more responsible act than one would expect of him. His treatment of the bewildered Fanny is anything but kind, however, and Hardy arranges for Troy to regret bitterly his harshness.

Hardy's concept of a brooding Fate that controls man's destiny is evident in poor Fanny's mistake in locating the right church. The names of the two churches are quite similar, and this small mischance helps to cause Fanny's final sufferings and guides the outcome of the events of the rest of the novel.

CHAPTER XVII: IN THE MARKET-PLACE

Boldwood sees Bathsheba enter the Casterbridge market on Saturday. Since her last visit here, Boldwood's feelings have changed remarkably. He had ignored her before, but curiosity about the sender of the valentine causes him to examine her more closely. He thinks she is quite beautiful but wonders if he is wrong, since the men at the market treat her casually. He asks a neighbor if Bathsheba is considered a beauty and is satisfied that he is not wrong. He wonders why she had done so strange a thing as sending him the valentine, and if she has any interest in him.

As he watches Bathsheba talking with a young farmer, he realizes he is jealous and longs to interrupt them. Bathsheba is aware of his attention and feels a sense of triumph in capturing his interest. She hardly considers Boldwood as a serious choice for a husband, and is genuinely sorry for her foolishness in sending him the valentine. She resolves to apologize the next time they meet, but at the same time thinks that the apology is as bad as the original joke.If he thought she was laughing at him, the apology would be even more insulting; if he took her seriously, he would see the apology as another example of her calling attention to herself.

Comment

The way for Boldwood's fall into the devastating obsession to win Bathsheba had been prepared by his aborted visit, and her foolish valentine. He knows little about his new neighbor; in fact, he knows little about women and must inquire of another man if she is considered beautiful.

The Biblical **allusion** to Adam's first sight of Eve is a brilliant comment on the action here. Like Adam, Boldwood is to be betrayed by his new Eve; but unlike Adam, Boldwood only glimpses Paradise, and never really enjoys it.

CHAPTER XVIII: BOLDWOOD IN MEDITATION - REGRET

Boldwood is a respected member of the community, and his gentlemanly style makes him the closest thing to aristocracy or landed gentry that the village can claim. He lives a solitary life as tenant farmer on Little Weatherbury farm; his prosperity is shown in his stock of fine horses. After the horses had been fed, Boldwood would often pace up and down the barn and meditate until dark.

It appears Boldwood is a rather reserved person, but in fact he has fine control of his emotions. If his peaceful life is disturbed by any outside force, he is apt to react violently. He has little sense of humor and is usually rather serious. When Bathsheba sent her teasing valentine, she little realized what an effect it could have on a person like Boldwood.

On an early spring day, during the time when the sheep are set out to graze, Boldwood looks across the level fields to Bathsheba's farm and sees Bathsheba with Gabriel and Cainy Bell. As he recognizes Bathsheba, Boldwood's face betrays his feelings; he plans to speak to her. His long period of isolation from love is over; his passion for her can no longer be contained.

Bathsheba and Gabriel are engaged in the task of getting a sheep to "adopt" one of the twins of another ewe, as a substitute for its own dead lamb. As Bathsheba looks up to see Boldwood at the gate, she blushes, and Gabriel, noticing her change of expression, turns to see the visitor. He realizes that this meeting has something to do with Bathsheba's letter, and that she has been toying with Boldwood's feelings in some way.

Boldwood understands that the two are aware of his presence, and he becomes confused. He is overcome by shyness and is hesitant to speak. He is unused to courting practices, and his inexperience in love and wooing makes him uncertain of his actions and of her response to his visit.

On the other hand, Bathsheba is sure that Boldwood has not come this way accidentally, or on a specific errand. She is quite troubled by his attention to her and promises herself never to encourage him in any way, but the consequences of her foolishness have been too firmly set to be altered now.

Comment

Hardy slows the action of the story in order to draw a more precise picture of Boldwood. It is important to remember that Boldwood seems calm and quite controlled, but might act violently if provoked. His sudden passion for Bathsheba is easily explained, if the reader recalls that he has firmly controlled his emotions for years until the shock of receiving the valentine brought their release.

CHAPTER XIX: THE SHEEP-WASHING - THE OFFER

Eventually Boldwood does call on Bathsheba, but she is not at home. Since he is a farmer himself, Boldwood understands that her busy life as manager of the farm leaves her little time for social life. His failure to see her, however, causes him to further idealize her in his imagination, and, by the end of May, he is determined to find out her feelings for him.

When he asks for her at the farmhouse, he is told that she is at the sheep-washing; at a circular, basin-like pool, several of her workers, including Gabriel, are herding her flock of sheep through the pool to wash away any dirt or impurities from their valuable fleeces. It is a perfect spring day; the meadows and trees never seemed greener. Bathsheba looks her best in an elegant new riding habit, as she watches the washing operation.

Boldwood greets her and Bathsheba leaves the pool to gain more privacy in her talk with him. As they near a bend in the nearby river, Boldwood calls to her and she stops to wait for him. He asks her to marry him, and she tries to remain composed as he describes his feelings for her. Trying to remain as dignified as he is, Bathsheba replies that she respects him, but does not love him, and is not justified in accepting his proposal.

Boldwood's passion breaks his control; he begs her to let him repeat his statement of love and to listen to his pleas. He has been able to make the decision to marry her partly because her valentine message indicated an interest in him. He is willing to marry her, even if she does not love him. Bathsheba again refuses and tries to explain her action as thoughtless. Boldwood has become so obsessed with the idea of winning her that he will not listen to any refusal. He promises her anything she wants, if she will only accept.

Although she is sympathetic, and feels responsible for causing his suffering, Bathsheba cannot return his love. She begs him to give her time to think. Boldwood presses her not to refuse absolutely and to allow him to speak to her again about marriage. She grants him this permission, but warns him not to hope for her. After she leaves, Boldwood stands as if stunned, until he returns to a sense of reality and abruptly returns to his home.

Comment

This is only the first of Bathsheba's painful confrontations with Boldwood; her foolish desire to be admired, without committing herself in any way (as if she were a rose, or a work of art created only to be viewed behind an enclosure) is not natural, indeed even inhuman, and she is forced to accept the consequences of her folly. Her pride must be humbled, and she must realize that she is mortal and part of the human community, before she can find true happiness.

CHAPTER XX: PERPLEXITY - GRINDING THE SHEARS - A QUARREL

Bathsheba weighs Boldwood's proposal objectively. She feels that he is kind in promising her so much; the match is socially desirable, and he is a respected man in Weatherbury. If she thought of marriage for its own sake, Boldwood would make an excellent husband, but she neither wants, nor loves him. In addition, she enjoys managing her farm, and does not wish to give up her independence. She is still uneasy about her part in encouraging Boldwood, and so she seeks out Gabriel (who is grinding shears for the sheep shearing) to get his opinion.

She sends Cainy Bell away and turns the grindstone for a few minutes, and then asks Gabriel to let her hold the shears so that she might talk to him. She is curious about the rustics' reaction to her talk with Boldwood, but Gabriel keeps her attention on the shears. In reply to her questions, Gabriel reports that not only did the men think the meeting an odd one, but also they expected Bathsheba and Boldwood to be married within a year.

She cries out that the idea is foolish and that she has come to ask Gabriel to control the rumor. Gabriel is surprised and relieved by the news, but rejects Bathsheba's request to spread the story that Boldwood had not proposed.

Bathsheba corrects him for calling her by her first name, and insists that the marriage will not take place. She is torn between pity for him (as a disappointed lover) and anger (that he has stopped loving her). Since she values his honesty and frankness, she asks his opinion of the situation. He tells her that her actions were not suited to any thoughtful, worthy woman, and adds that she probably resents his rudeness. Bathsheba is angry at the truth of his evaluation and dismisses his rebuke as best she can, but loses her temper. Stung by his candor, she orders him to leave the farm at the end of the week. Gabriel calmly replies that he'd rather leave at once. She angrily orders him not to let her see his face again. Gabriel agrees and leaves her, moving with calm dignity.

Comment

Bathsheba meets her match in independence in Gabriel, but his independence is tempered by a maturity she has not yet achieved. She half-expects his answers and opinions, yet asks them; she is accustomed to flattery, or strongly wishes for it, and finds Gabriel's frankness annoying. She is like a petulant child when she orders him from the farm; the allusion to Moses leaving the presence of the Pharaoh is almost mock-epic in the context.

Gabriel is of course patient and understanding with his difficult mistress; he is perfectly aware that she is still too young to judge fairly. He never loses his dignity, even when faced with her "tantrum."

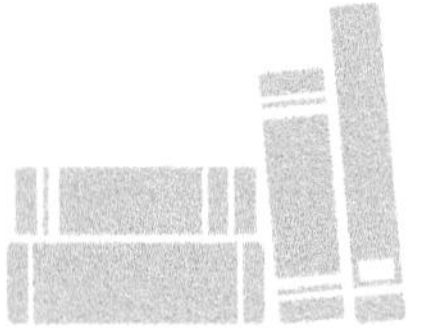

FAR FROM THE MADDING CROWD

TEXTUAL ANALYSIS

CHAPTERS 21-30

CHAPTER XXI: TROUBLES IN THE FOLD - A MESSAGE

Bathsheba's triumph over Gabriel is short-lived. The next day her sheep wander into a field of clover and are blasted. Bathsheba scolds her workers for not getting the sheep out of the field sooner; as they talk, several sheep fall down in the field, seriously injured.

Tall remarks that the only way of saving them is to pierce their sides with a special instrument, and that Gabriel is the only man skillful enough to perform the operation. Bathsheba at first refuses to send for Gabriel, but the prospect of dead and dying sheep forces her to humble herself. She sends Laban Tall for Gabriel; she worries that he may already have left. Gabriel, however, sends back word that he will not come until she makes her request politely; when another sheep dies, Bathsheba hurries to the house to write Gabriel a note, including the words, "Do not desert me, Gabriel!" Anxiously, they all await the outcome; Gabriel finally appears without any sign of his small victory. She reproaches him, but gently, and Gabriel is confused by her change of manner. He hurries to the field and saves the sheep by inserting a small tube, which allows the air surplus to escape. When the sheep are out of danger, Bathsheba, confident that he still loves her, asks Gabriel to stay, and he agrees.

Comment

Bathsheba's independence is slowly waning, as she acknowledges her need for Gabriel. On the other hand, he establishes his independence of her; when he returns to the farm, it is on his own terms, and a new relationship with her is established.

It is ironic that Bathsheba is forced to send for Gabriel, the day after she dismissed him. The rustics are comic in their perplexity, but they manage to agree on one thing: Gabriel is the only possible savior for the flock. Bathsheba is forced to accept the situation and send for Gabriel.

Gabriel, in his own way enjoys the situation. In accord with his conscience, and his perception of "things as they should be," he waits until he is properly requested to come. He declares a kind of independence by this act, but Bathsheba has not lost her hold over him, as is shown by his pleasure at her welcome and at her smiles.

CHAPTER XXII: THE GREAT BARN AND THE SHEEP-SHEARERS

On the first of June, the village people gather to help shear the sheep in the great barn. The old barn, resembling either a church or a castle, is well suited for the operation. Modern techniques are still far from Weatherbury, and the shearing is performed as it had been many years before. Weatherbury seems unaffected by the passing of the years and actually seems to resist change.

The rustics are supervised at the various tasks by Bathsheba, assisted by Gabriel, who seems to be the manager of the entire procedure. Bathsheba watches him as he shears a sheep; Gabriel is silently content to have her attention and to listen to her chatter. The shorn sheep is marked by Cainy with Bathsheba's initials, and the fleece is taken away and placed with the others. Gabriel's happiness at the progress of the work and with Bathsheba's presence is marred by the appearance of Boldwood. He and Bathsheba talk in low tones, and Gabriel is sure that their conversation does not involve sheep-shearing. Bathsheba leaves the barn and returns dressed in a new riding habit.

As he prepares to ride away with Boldwood, Gabriel is so upset that he accidentally cuts a sheep. Bathsheba scolds him and Gabriel realizes that she is upset about something more than the sheep. She tells Gabriel that she is going to see Boldwood's stock, and leaves him in charge. The laborers comment on the significance of the visit. Henery fails to see why such an independent woman needs a husband. Henery is still annoyed that he has not been chosen as bailiff; he reports that he thinks Boldwood kissed Bathsheba at the sheep washing. Oak springs to Bathsheba's defense, but Henery insists that his judgment is to be trusted, and that he is just as clever as Gabriel. Somehow the malster fancies himself slighted, and both he and Henery must be pacified. The mood is lightened when Maryann asks if there is any man available for her to marry. Gabriel continues to work quietly; Bathsheba had hinted that he was to be bailiff and he looked forward to the post, not for its advancement, but for its closer relationship with her. If she marries Boldwood, the whole situation would change. However badly she treats him, he still loves her and is anxious to help her. Cainy interrupts his thoughts and brings his attention back to the work and the feast to follow. Poorgrass especially is looking forward to the eating and drinking, since his body particularly needs "nourishment."

Comment

Despite the complexity of the Boldwood-Bathsheba-Gabriel relationships in the chapter, the impression of calm serenity in the village of Weatherbury is maintained. The village remains relatively the same; fifty years have no meaning for its inhabitants. The rustics labor at the same tasks, and in the same way, that their forefathers had. Although Hardy realized that villages like Weatherbury had disappeared, or were being depopulated, his lasting respect for them, and for the tradition they represented, is particularly evident and herein expressed extremely well.

CHAPTER XXIII: EVENTIDE - A SECOND DECLARATION

A long table for the shearing supper is drawn up to the farmhouse; one end is set inside the parlor window, so that Bathsheba sits at the head of the table, but not with her workers. Even the presence of the unwelcome dismissed bailiff, Pennyways, does not dim her excitement; she asks Gabriel to assist her by sitting at the bottom of the table and acting as a host to the workers near him. Boldwood arrives shortly after, however, and Bathsheba asks Gabriel to give him his place; Gabriel silently gives up his seat to the farmer, who seems unusually happy and gay.

After the supper, Coggan begins the singing, to be followed by Poorgrass, with a song of his own composing. Young Coggan is so overcome by laughter at the "ballet" that his father reprimands him, but Poorgrass is so insulted that he will not continue. Jacob Smallbury restores peace by starting a seemingly endless **ballad**. Even after sundown the merriment continues; Bathsheba, now occupied with her knitting, surveys that scene from her window. Gabriel misses Boldwood from his place at the table, and, as Liddy lights the candles inside the house, Gabriel sees Boldwood sitting near Bathsheba.

The rustics request a song from Bathsheba; she asks Gabriel to accompany her on his flute and sings a song with a verse referring to a soldier and his ride. Boldwood joins in the song, and the rustics enjoy the performance in complete silence. Gabriel observes Boldwood's actions toward Bathsheba and the rustics, and guesses that Boldwood's position seems more secure.

Bathsheba bids them all good-night and closes the window and shutter. Oak leaves, and the rustics begin to follow, complimenting Pennyways on his "return" to honesty.

Inside the house, Boldwood has been urging Bathsheba to marry him. She promises to try to love him and to marry him, if she thinks she could make him a good wife, but she will not give him a solemn promise that night. She refuses to promise anything more than that, at the end of five or six weeks, she will probably be able to promise to marry him.

Boldwood is satisfied as he leaves. Bathsheba is ashamed of her past behavior and very impressed by Boldwood's love. Her joke may have brought rave consequences, but she finds a kind of pleasure in her conquest of such a man as Boldwood.

Comment

The intensity of the Boldwood-Bathsheba relationship is offset by Gabriel's calm study of the two, and the gaiety of the rustics. Hardy gives the reader a good view of the simplicity of the rustics' pleasure: goodnatured banter and songs that are old favorites. They are goodhearted enough to accept Pennyways back into their community and to readily forgive him his crimes, since he is apparently making restitution. The chapter also offers us an insight into the easy relationship between Bathsheba and her workers; each knows his place, and the harmony is evident in their asking a song of Bathsheba, and her acceptance.

The song itself is a good example of Hardy's use of **irony** and his development of suspense. Bathsheba sings of a soldier with a "winning tongue" who seeks a bride. Hardy tells us that many of those present will remember the gay bride and the clever soldier, but does not say whether the memory will be pleasant or bitter. The hint of the soldier, and some connection between him and Bathsheba's story, serves as an intriguing introduction of Troy in the next chapter.

CHAPTER XXIV: THE SAME NIGHT - THE FIR PLANTATION

Since Bathsheba had dismissed the bailiff and had taken over the management of the farm herself, she had assumed the task of inspecting the farm grounds at night. She made these trips with a dark lantern, turning it on occasionally to examine some dark corner. Although she was fairly safe, and the farm so well managed that very little could be found wrong, Gabriel usually made his own inspection before Bathsheba did, without allowing her to know about it.

On the night of the shearing feast, she made her customary inspection. Only the usual barnyard sounds disturbed the peaceful stillness of the night. She makes her way back to the house by a path through a group of fir trees; the thick needles and branches made this path seem to be a passage through a long, dark hall. Even though the darkness made this path a possible danger point, Bathsheba usually found it safe. This time, however, she is startled to hear the sound of footsteps from the other end. She assures herself that the unknown person is probably a villager returning home, and regrets meeting him at the darkest point of her own walk. As the two are about to pass each other, Bathsheba feels something tug at her skirt and is nearly thrown off balance.

A man's voice asks if she has been hurt and explains that they have somehow become entangled. He asks for her lantern, and Bathsheba is startled to see a soldier revealed by the sudden light. His spur has caught on her long skirt; Bathsheba refuses his offer to unfasten it, but the rowel of the spur has wound itself so firmly, that she has difficulty in setting herself free. He bends to try to help her, and his movement allows her to notice that he is young, handsome, and a sergeant. Although he thinks the dress may have to be cut away from the spur, he continues trying to unravel the threads, using the time to coolly examine Bathsheba's face and to comment on her beauty.

His compliments confuse her, but she realizes that he has been delaying his task purposely. She is afraid that a sudden wrench would further damage her skirt, or worse still, pull it from her. The soldier continues his compliments, until she finally manages to separate the skirt from the spur. He explains that he is no stranger to the area and identifies himself as Sergeant Troy. Carefully inching past him, she moves slowly down the path, and then hurries into the house to question Liddy about him.

Liddy reports that Troy has a reputation for being a gay, clever young dandy. He is said to have had a good education and to be descended from nobility, but he seems to be wasting his opportunities by enlisting as a soldier. Despite her better convictions, Bathsheba begins to be charmed by the soldier and actually accuses herself of not being too polite to the young man. She is rather pleased by his compliments; while Boldwood might be a determined lover, he never complimented her beauty.

Comment

Hardy has prepared the reader for the introduction of Troy very craftily with Bathsheba's song in the previous chapter. Troy has the same winning tongue as the soldier of the song; he uses his clever words to charm Bathsheba. We already know of her vanity and her desire for admiration, and it is not surprising to see how readily she accepts Troy's compliments, despite her embarrassment and her fundamental good sense.

The **episode** of the entangling of her skirt and Troy's spur is obviously contrived, but it allows Bathsheba and Troy to become acquainted and makes her a "captive audience" for his compliments. The setting is "romantic," a dark isolated path which seems perfect for some exciting adventure to unfold.

CHAPTER XXV: THE NEW ACQUAINTANCE DESCRIBED

A character sketch of Troy takes up most of this chapter. He lives constantly in the present, never caring for the future, or worrying about the past. He is never disappointed, since he has few hopes; his honesty is "divided," he is fairly truthful with men, but feels free to lie to women. His vices seem minor or excusable (since he is still a young man); his wrongdoing results from acting impulsively, while he is rarely seen in a virtuous act.

He seems very active, but his acts are inspired by the heat of the moment, and as the heat cools, his plans and work cool with it. However quick his understanding and strong his character, he had little force of will. He is well-educated for a soldier and gifted in flattering speeches (especially to women); almost unconsciously he can spin flattering comments, and he hardly ever considers their impact.

A week or two after the shearing, Bathsheba, feeling rather relieved at Boldwood's absence, goes out to the hayfields to watch the haymakers. In one section, the hay is already being loaded; Troy works with the others, as if he were a knight offering his services to his lady-love. Troy notices her as soon as she comes into the field; he walks toward her, leaving his hayfork on the ground. Bathsheba blushes and focuses her eyes on her path.

Comment

The description of Troy is almost directly opposite that of Gabriel; Troy is everything Gabriel is not. Troy's honesty and dependability is imperfect; he is impulsive, and pretends to be upright and moral only when the occasion suits him. He enjoys flattering pretty women, and is quite expert at clever phrases, since he practices very often. He is like Bathsheba in one respect; he never weighs the outcome of his actions or remarks. Hardy points out the falseness of Troy's character even in the **episode** at the hayfield; Troy is not helping the haymakers for any serious reasons, but seems merely to want to impress Bathsheba. The alert reader recognizes what Gabriel sees-Troy is rarely what he seems to be.

CHAPTER XXVI: SCENE ON THE VERGE OF THE HAY-MEAD

Troy addresses Bathsheba as "Queen of the Cornmarket," and apologizes for his very free conduct during their first meeting. He manages to turn his apologies into more compliments. Bathsheba feels that his freedom should be checked, but rather enjoys his compliments and finds it hard to be rude to him. In spite of himself, she laughs at his remarks, as he explains that since he adores only pretty women his religious worship is restricted. His compliments completely captivate her, and Troy notices the effect of his remarks.

He continues his task of winning her and says that he would be conceited to think she had any interest in him. Bathsheba agrees that he is conceited, but Troy carefully steers from a discussion of his faults to his pleasure in her conversation. He insists that he fell in love with her at first sight; Bathsheba tells him that this is impossible and tries to break off the conversation. When she asks him the time, he tries to present her with a gold watch that is an heirloom in the family of the Earls of Severn. He begs her to keep it and assures her that he will be pleased to think she has the watch; by this time his statements have become more serious than he himself realized. She returns the watch and agrees to allow him to call on her during the rest of his stay. Bathsheba is so distracted and so excited by his compliments that she leaves the hayfield, unable to face the haymakers. She wonders what the significance of this meeting might be, and how much of Troy's remarks she can believe.

Comment

This chapter might well be named "The Winning of Bathsheba." Practiced as he is in the art of wooing, Troy immediately chooses exactly the right manner to gain her favor. He compliments her beauty and charm and asks little in return: her approval and her company. The approach is perfect; Bathsheba thinks she has found someone who can give her the compliments she enjoys, without asking anything more than her permission to admire her. Her common sense begins to desert her; she can hardly summon up enough strength to resist accepting the watch.

Troy, however, is also caught in his own trap. His clever speeches and dramatic gestures (such as impulsively offering her his watch) enable him to win her interest, but Troy finds himself being more serious about his admission of love than he at first realized. Bathsheba's beauty and charm have won him, and this meeting is a turning point in both of their lives.

CHAPTER XXVII: HIVING THE BEES

Late in June, Bathsheba watches a swarm of bees settling in the orchard. Many times the bees have been quite "cooperative" and have settled in low branches, making it easy for a worker to catch the bees in a hive. This year, as has happened before, however, they have been late in swarming and have chosen a high bough which was difficult to reach which meant that ladders and long poles had to be used.

Since most of her workers were busy at the haymaking, Bathsheba decides to hive the bees herself. She dons gloves, a large hat and a heavy veil and climbs up the ladder, only to be stopped by Troy's arrival. She hurries back down the ladder and drops the hive. Troy offers to shake the bees into the hive for her; she insists that he wear the protective veil, hat and gloves. His appearance in this attire is so ridiculous that she starts to laugh, and their relationship becomes even more informal. While he is busy with his work, she uses the time to freshen her appearance. He finishes the hiving and descends from the tree; he asks her help in untying the veil. To ease the embarrassment of this close contact, she asks about his demonstration of the sword exercise.

She had heard accounts of his skill in handling a sword; she would like to see a performance. He promises to give her an exhibition, if she will wait until the evening, since he must arrange to get a sword. He urges her to meet him; when she cautiously suggests bringing Liddy, he coldly refuses. She is anxious to see the exercise - and perhaps to meet him - and agrees to come.

Comment

Hardy's familiarity with rustic customs and duties is again in evidence in this chapter. For the simple villagers of Weatherbury, the passing of the various seasons is noted not necessarily by changes in the weather, but by the varied tasks performed at different times of the year. The spring means the time for washing the sheep, the summer brings shearing, haymaking and hiving the bees. Hardy takes advantage of this calendar to match the developments of his story; since Bathsheba and Troy's relationship grows in the summer, their love assumes a summer quality, intense, but short-lived.

CHAPTER XXVIII: THE HOLLOW AMID THE FERNS

At eight o'clock that evening, Bathsheba makes her way toward a plot of land near a hill opposite her home. This section was full of tall groups of ferns; in one place the earth formed a natural valley, surrounded by ferns. She pauses and starts for home again; when she thinks how disappointed the sergeant will be, she decides to meet him, as she promised. Troy greets her as she reaches this tiny valley and produces his sword.

He starts the sword drill, explaining his movements as he performs. Bathsheba enjoys watching the blade flash in the setting sun; her adventurous spirit is excited by the display, and she overcomes any qualms she has about this odd meeting as she becomes absorbed in the performance. Troy tests her courage by quickly flashing the sword around her. She is frightened that she might be hurt, but Troy's skill leaves her unharmed. He warns her to stand very still and Bathsheba is thrilled by the whistle and gleam of the circling blade. He climaxes his display by neatly cutting off a lock of her hair, and compliments her bravery. He urges her to let him continue and kills a caterpillar that was crawling on the front of her dress, without her even feeling the point of the sword. He insists that she was perfectly safe, despite the razor-sharp edge of the sword, since his swordsmanship was so perfect.

As she sits down on some heather, Troy tells her he must leave and that he will keep the lock of her hair as a memento. He puts it away carefully, and as he comes close to taking his leave, bends down and kisses her. Bathsheba, overcharged with emotion and feeling a bit guilty, bursts into tears.

Comment

The sword exercise is a good indication of Troy's appeal; he is so different from anyone she has ever known. His manly skill gives him an adventurous, foreign air; he is totally confident in his skill and is bold enough to risk her life to prove it. In comparing this talent to Gabriel's devoted and practical abilities in caring for his sheep, Troy's experience seems more glamorous, but far less useful and beneficial.

Troy's ability to handle his sword well causes an emotional rather than a rational response in Bathsheba; his performance thrills and frightens (like a dangerous circus act), and precludes an objective testing. At this point, however, Bathsheba is not interested in patient and careful study (such as Gabriel would require), and is immediately captivated by Troy's strong emotional appeal.

CHAPTER XXIX: PARTICULARS OF A TWILIGHT WALK

Against her better judgment and instinctive recognition of his weakness, Bathsheba finds herself in love with Troy. The love is far from rational, and if any other woman presented the circumstances of their relationship to her, Bathsheba would probably advise her against further involvement. Bathsheba is too overcome by her own feelings to be able to analyze her attachment to Troy. She could speak to Liddy about Boldwood, since she felt only respect for him; her love for Troy had to be kept to herself.

Gabriel is aware of her infatuation and feels quite troubled by it; not only because of his own love for Bathsheba, but because he recognizes Troy's weakness of character. He takes the opportunity to talk to Bathsheba about her treatment of Boldwood when he meets her one evening, as she is returning from a walk. Bathsheba denies that she will marry Boldwood and Gabriel can no longer restrain himself from expressing his opinions. He points out that Boldwood's courtship was widely known and that the villagers were confident of an early wedding date. Bathsheba strongly defends her position; she respects Boldwood and he has urged this marriage, but she refuses to accept his proposal. Gabriel blames Troy for ruining Boldwood's hopes and warns her that Troy is not to be trusted; her reputation might be ruined by her association with Troy.

Bathsheba eagerly defends Troy and explains that his modesty hides his good works; she uses, as an example of this, Troy's habit of entering church by an old tower door and seating himself, unnoticed, in the rear. Gabriel is distressed at her strong defense of Troy and at her attachment to him.

Gabriel assures her that he still loves her, but, for the sake of her reputation, begs her to marry Boldwood. She angrily orders him from the farm, but he dismisses this order as if it came from a child. He tells her that he is tired of helping her through troubles she causes for herself, and he agrees to leave if she will hire a responsible man to help her manage the farm. He adds that she should feel grateful for his staying on, since he could raise his own position if he should decide to leave. He continues to work for her only because of his devotion for her; he apologizes for his abruptness and insists that he is only concerned for her happiness. Although she is secretly delighted by his faithfulness, she sends him away. Gabriel worries about leaving her in such a deserted area, but he sees Troy join her and he hurries home. He passes the churchyard on his way and notices that the tower door (supposedly used by Troy) was so undisturbed by use that ivy grew across it.

Comment

Hardy subtly underscores Troy's dishonesty and lack of sincerity with the **episode** of the unused tower door. It was just like Troy to lie about his church-going without bothering to see if his lie could be detected. It is quite ironic that Gabriel is the one to discover Troy's lie; Gabriel is still clear-sighted enough to detect it, for Bathsheba is so blinded by Troy's deceitful charm that she would probably never notice the unused door.

CHAPTER XXX: HOT CHEEKS AND TEARFUL EYES

Bathsheba arrives home excited, but also a bit sad. Troy had kissed her again, as he said good night, but he also told her that he was leaving to visit friends at Bath. She feels she must write Boldwood and firmly refuse his offer of marriage. She had intended to wait for Boldwood's return from a short trip to tell him this, but now she wants him to have the letter as soon as possible.

As she walks to the kitchen to find someone to deliver her note, she hears her women servants discussing her marriage to Troy. She bursts into the kitchen and questions the women about their gossiping; they admit that the talk concerned her. She insists that she has no interest in Troy, but gives herself away by continuing to defend him. She warns them that she will dismiss anyone who speaks against him. She leaves the letter and hurries back to the parlor, scarcely able to control her emotions. Liddy follows and tries to apologize; she promises that she will refute any future gossip by stating that Bathsheba is too much of a lady to be in love with Troy.

Bathsheba surprises Liddy by revealing that she indeed does love Troy; she regrets her denial of her love and asks Liddy to swear that Troy does have a good reputation. Liddy's hesitation angers Bathsheba; by this time Liddy is thoroughly confused by Bathsheba's rapid changes of temperament, but finally promises to think well of Troy to keep their conversation a secret. She has been so upset by this exchange that she announces that she will leave Bathsheba's service.

Bathsheba pacifies her by telling her that she is more companion than servant; Liddy's departure would leave Bathsheba without a friend. The two rejoice over their renewed friendship, but Liddy asks Bathsheba to try to control the violence of her passionate feelings about Troy. She finds this an intensely female trait in Bathsheba and mourns her own lack of it.

Comment

Troy's notorious reputation is well known by the villagers; they are far from blinded by his charm. Unlike Gabriel, Troy has no friends among the villagers; up to this point in the story, it seems that his only friends are female.

Bathsheba's women servants are especially understanding of Troy and his hold over Bathsheba. They are not necessarily malicious in their gossip, but since they are not involved in a relationship with Troy, they can manage to see him realistically and to accept the stories about him as truthful.

FAR FROM THE MADDING CROWD

TEXTUAL ANALYSIS

CHAPTERS 31-40

CHAPTER XXXI: BLAME - FURY

Bathsheba wishes to avoid any meeting with Boldwood, so, on the following evening, she prepares to take advantage of Liddy's invitation to visit her married sister. Liddy has been given a week's holiday, and Bathsheba decides to join her at Yalbury for a day or two. She leaves Gabriel and Maryann in charge of the farm and, just after a thunderstorm had freshened the surrounding area, leaves the house. She enjoys her pleasant walk, until Boldwood suddenly appears in her path. He looks totally unlike his former self and he is so occupied with his thoughts that he does not notice Bathsheba until they actually meet.

He asks her if she is afraid of him, even though he loves her; Bathsheba tries to comfort him and to continue on her way. Boldwood prolongs the meeting by questioning her about the finality of her decision and then by asking for her pity. Bathsheba manages to control her behavior under these difficult circumstances, but Boldwood seems nearly mad as he pleads with her. He reminds her that she first encouraged his interest, that she is the first woman he ever loved, and that she had so nearly promised to marry him that his pain is now doubly severe. She agrees that her valentine was a poor joke and explains that she did not realize that what might be an idle flirtation for other men was a serious matter to him. His repeated reproaches and charges, as well as pleas for her pity, upset Bathsheba and she tries to calm him. She asks him to forgive her and to accept the situation cheerfully. He finds this suggestion heartless; he is still torn between rejecting her forever and begging her to accept him.

She tries to explain that, although she is not hard-hearted, she finds it difficult to love anyone. He refuses to see her as a cold woman, however, and tells her that he knows that she loves Troy. He turns his anger on the soldier for robbing him of Bathsheba; when she admits she loves Troy, he regrets having fallen in love with her, and having lost his honor and reputation.

She is so terrified by his words and conduct that she reminds him that she is only an unprotected girl; his conduct, she contends, is ungentlemanly. Boldwood forces her to admit that Troy had kissed her; he curses Troy and prophesies that someday Troy will have to repent and feel as miserable as he (Boldwood) does now. Despite Bathsheba's pleas for Troy, Boldwood vows to punish him; he regrets blaming Bathsheba and now directs his wrath and disappointment at his successful rival.

Bathsheba is shocked by the man's violence; she had always known him as a reserved, quiet man. She is glad that Troy is at Bath, and not with his regiment, as generally supposed; she fears that his return would involve a disastrous meeting with Boldwood. She thinks Troy should be warned, but, on the other hand, he might think her foolish if she insisted on his danger. She sits down to consider the situation and ignores the signs of the approaching evening, intent only on Troy.

Comment

The half-deranged man who curses Troy is far from the cool, reserved gentleman that Bathsheba first saw at the Casterbridge market. His curse is tragically prophetic; Troy will suffer a loss similar to Boldwood's. Hardy opens a new line of suspense in the story with Boldwood's vow to punish Troy; the punishment will destroy them both.

CHAPTER XXXII: NIGHT - HORSES TRAMPING

The quiet peace of the night in Weatherbury, and on Bathsheba's farm, is disturbed around eleven o'clock by someone taking one of Bathsheba's horses and hitching it to a light carriage. Maryann is awakened by the noise and, when she sees the apparent robbery, hurries to report it at the nearest house, Coggan's. Coggan calls Gabriel to investigate, and the three hear the sound of the horse in the distance. Gabriel decides to ride after the robber and he and Coggan borrow two of Boldwood's horses, since none of Bathsheba's are suited for a chase. Coggan and Gabriel track the horse and carriage, long after the sound stopped directing them in their pursuit. They realize that the horse has gone lame; Gabriel is confident that they can easily catch up with the robber, since he will be delayed by the slow horse and by the sleepy gatekeeper at the turnpike.

Gabriel calls to the gatekeeper to stop the thief; he is surprised to discover Bathsheba driving the carriage. Bathsheba explains that she is on her way to Bath and asks what they are doing. She is upset that they have made such a mistake and had even borrowed Boldwood's horses; she had left a note in chalk on the coach-horse doors, but, of course, it was not visible at night. She realizes that she should be pleased by their sense of responsibility and she thanks them for all their efforts. Her horse has been temporarily lamed by picking up a stone in her shoe; Bathsheba sends them home and continues on towards Bath. Gabriel and Coggan agree to keep the **episode** secret.

After her meeting with Boldwood, Bathsheba had spent some time considering her problem. She had finally decided that she must warn Troy about Boldwood and, hard as it was, she must take Gabriel's advice and give up Troy. She began to feel sorry for herself but she made up her mind to search for Troy at once, foolishly promising herself that he would strengthen her in her resolve to break off their friendship. It is evident, however, that she was hoping she would at least see him once more. Although the journey to Bath would be difficult, especially since she would have to start at night, Bathsheba decides not to go on to visit Liddy and her sister, but to return to the farm and prepare for the longer trip. She planned to see Troy and take her leave of him, rest her horse, and then ride on to see Liddy. She hopes, in this way, to keep her visit to Bath a secret, but she had misjudged the distance, and her workers' suspicion of robbery had made this scheme a failure.

Comment

Hardy's skill in maintaining suspense for his magazine readers is again evident in this chapter which is similar in structure to Chapter VI. In both chapters Hardy hides the identity of a person who turns out to be Bathsheba. Whereas in the earlier chapter Gabriel fights the fire on her farm with her workers, in this one, the reader guesses that the rider Gabriel chases is Bathsheba, but her actual identification is not made until the **climax** of the chapter, which creates an effect of surprise similar to that of revealing Bathsheba as the young lady who owned Weatherbury Farm.

CHAPTER XXXIII: IN THE SUN - A HARBINGER

Bathsheba remains on at Bath for two weeks without any further explanation of her absence than a note to Maryann saying that she was still detained on the business which took her to Bath. The men begin the harvesting of the oats during a terrible drought. As they work, Maryann tells them that she has had a warning of some trouble; she had dropped the door key and broken it. Coggan and Gabriel, who is helping with the harvesting for Bathsheba's sake, see Cainy Bell running toward them. He has been away for a few days, since he had a finger infection, and could not help with the farm work. The villagers remark that only accidents like this give them time to enjoy some leisure.

All of the workers gather around Cainy to hear his news, but he is frustrated in telling his story, since his long run so soon after eating has caused him to choke. He finally manages to say that he has seen Bathsheba with a soldier, and that the two appeared to be a "courting couple." His choking, coughing and sneezing make the rustics impatient, and Coggan finally gives him some cider to relieve this difficulty. Cainy, however, drinks the cider so quickly that the drink only adds to his troubles; it spills over his clothes and keeps him sputtering and coughing. The interruptions by the villagers make poor Gabriel more impatient than ever to hear Cainy's story; Cainy finally manages to tell him that the very attentive soldier with Bathsheba was Sergeant Troy. Gabriel's curiosity about the two grows as the rustics question Cainy about Bath. He tells them of the customs of the inhabitants (their drinking of the famous spring water causes Matthew to comment on native customs seeming barbaric to outsiders), and of his own adventures in the city. Gabriel questions him about Bathsheba; Cainy describes how beautiful she looked as she strolled with the handsome soldier. He continues talking about Bath and its people and finally admits that he saw little more of Bathsheba. The men try to get him to swear that it really was she and Cainy insists that, although he won't swear to it, he is certain it was. Gabriel is naturally upset by the news and tries not to show his disappointment, but Coggan notices his reaction and tries to comfort him. He reminds Gabriel that since Bathsheba cannot be his, it makes no difference whose sweetheart she is. Gabriel replies that he has been telling himself the same thing.

Comment

The same technique of suspense is used in a totally different manner in this chapter. Hardy adds humor to spice the reader's interest in Bathsheba's visit to Troy. Cainy is no story teller; he mixes up his **episodes** and time and brings in irrelevant material. In addition, he keeps his listeners (and the reader) in suspense, since he takes so long to tell his story, as he suffers from coughs, choking, and his friends' misguided efforts to help. However amusing the manner of Cainy's narration might be, his news is still serious; the reader is additionally motivated to read on to discover what happened when Bathsheba met Troy in Bath.

CHAPTER XXXIV: HOME AGAIN - A TRICKSTER

That same evening, Gabriel is relieved to see Bathsheba return in her carriage with Liddy. He leans on Coggan's garden gate to watch the gathering darkness, until he is greeted by Boldwood. Boldwood asks for Bathsheba at her home, but he is told that she cannot see him; he decides that she has not forgiven him for his conduct at their last meeting. As he starts home, he sees Troy coming back to the village and is determined to speak to him.

Boldwood meets Troy carrying a carpet bag and introduces himself. He tells Troy that he feels that Troy has been treating Bathsheba badly; he also informs him that he is aware that Troy is supposed to marry Fanny. Troy notices Boldwood's severe manner (and the club-like stick he carries) and decides to endure his comments as patiently as possible. He tries to explain to Boldwood that he cannot marry Fanny; he suggests that he is too poor to accept the responsibility.

Boldwood accuses him of taking Bathsheba away from him and asks him to leave her alone. If he will do this and marry Fanny, Boldwood promises Troy fifty pounds at once and five hundred pounds for Fanny on her wedding day. Troy pretends to be interested but he reminds Boldwood that Fanny is only a servant. Boldwood produces the money and the sergeant accepts it; when he teases Boldwood by saying that he has only Troy's word to carry out the bargain, Boldwood reminds him that there is still five hundred pounds (plus an extra "bonus" for Fanny) waiting for him on his wedding day, and Troy would hardly want to lose that.

A sound of footsteps is heard on the road; Troy tells Boldwood that Bathsheba is coming to meet him, and that he will make his farewell. Bathsheba greets Troy very affectionately (as Boldwood listens to their conversation from his hiding place); she tells him that she will be alone in her house and expects him to visit her there. Troy promises her he will join her in a few minutes; after she leaves, Troy teases Boldwood about his strange bargain. Troy really prefers Fanny, and now Boldwood has made this match worthwhile. Boldwood leaps to attack him; Troy manages to save his life by reminding him that Bathsheba would really suffer if he was harmed.

Now Boldwood insists that Troy marry Bathsheba, or her reputation will be ruined. He promises to pay Troy the five hundred pounds at once, and agrees to give him an additional twenty-one pounds that he has with him. Troy insists that they call on Bathsheba, and when they reach her house, he goes inside for a candle. He hands Boldwood a newspaper to read by the light of the candle and points out a paragraph which announces Troy's marriage to Bathsheba.

He ridicules Boldwood's schemes; he adds that, as bad as he is, he would never allow a woman to be a matter of sale in a marriage. He reveals that Fanny has been missing for some time, although he has searched everywhere for her. He further ridicules Boldwood's love, by pointing out that Boldwood was ready to believe the worst about her on very little evidence. He feels that he has taught Boldwood a lesson, and throws the money into the road.

Boldwood angrily shouts at him for playing such a trick and promises to punish him someday. Troy merely laughs at him and locks himself inside the house, as Boldwood leaves to walk around Weatherbury's hills and valleys all night long.

Comment

A good contrast in character is shown in Boldwood's bargain. He instinctively knows that a man like Troy could be bribed; he offers the money generously to save Bathsheba from him and to maintain both her good reputation and Fanny's. Troy seems to reject the money contemptuously, but had he not married Bathsheba and been secure in a position of importance on a prosperous farm, he might well have accepted the money as a "bonus" for marrying Fanny.

He seems to have an almost diabolic nature as he teases Boldwood first about accepting the money, and, even more cruelly, when he lets him think that Bathsheba has invited Troy for a private visit late at night, and does not reveal that Bathsheba and he have been married at Bath.

CHAPTER XXXV: AT AN UPPER WINDOW

Very early the next morning, Gabriel and Coggan walk toward Bathsheba's house and see Troy apparently well at ease, leaning out of an upper window. Coggan remarks that Bathsheba has evidently married Troy; he notices that Gabriel has turned very pale and tells him to try to control his reaction. Gabriel is quite distressed by this hasty marriage; he wonders why it was arranged so secretly, since Bathsheba's frank nature would have indicated a much more public wedding.

Troy greets the two men cheerfully; Gabriel refuses to answer, until Coggan reminds him that Troy is now master of the farm. Gabriel realizes that he must make the best of this unpleasant situation; he is not comforted, or even hopeful, when Coggan suggests that perhaps Bathsheba is not at home, and they have been wrong about the marriage. Troy delays them as he comments on the changes he will make and on his plans for modernization.

The two men are surprised to hear Troy ask Coggan if there has been any history of insanity in Boldwood's family. Coggan has heard some rumors, but he is not certain. Troy dismisses the idea lightly and tosses them a coin to drink his health, but Gabriel refuses it.

Coggan again warns Gabriel not to allow his feelings about Troy to become too obvious. He thinks that Troy will soon buy his discharge from the army and take over at the farm. Gabriel replies that if his place on the farm requires flattering Troy, he would rather leave the farm.

As they walk along, Boldwood appears on his horse, and the two move back to let him pass. Gabriel wonders what Troy meant by his question about Boldwood; his own grief is forgotten in seeing the effect of the news upon that one time reserved gentleman. His terrible suffering is obvious in his painfully controlled movements, as he rides towards his home.

Comment

The **episodes** in this chapter seem to echo those of the preceding one. The Boldwood-Troy confrontation is replaced by a meeting between Troy and Gabriel. Troy seems to be triumphant in both chapters and over both rivals. Of course, Gabriel's calm, philosophical acceptance is sharply contrasted with Boldwood's wild behavior. No bargaining takes place in this chapter, to be sure; but the echo of Troy's tossing Boldwood's money back at him can be heard in Troy's rather arrogant gift of a coin for drinks. Troy's plans for the farm indicate how far from a "natural" or farm-loving man he is; Gabriel accepts the traditional farm life with love and respect.

In addition, Hardy manages to give the reader a small hint about Boldwood's eventual tragedy. He describes Boldwood's actions and manner as half-insane or "deranged"; Troy inquires about madness in Boldwood's family. Slowly, the reader is being prepared for Boldwood's collapse.

CHAPTER XXXVI: WEALTH IN JEOPARDY - THE REVEL

At the end of August, Gabriel stands in the yard where the ricks are stored. His careful observations of the sky and the earth reveal that a terrible storm is on the way. He is concerned as he looks at the eight unprotected ricks which represent the produce from one-half the farm for that year.

It was this night that Troy, now master of the farm, was giving a harvest supper and dance. As Gabriel approaches the barn, he sees the gay decorations and the dancing now in progress. Troy welcomes the choice of the next selection, "The Soldier's Joy," since he has just received his discharge from the army. When this merry dance is finished, Gabriel sends word to Troy that he would like to speak to him, but Troy refuses to come. Gabriel, who cannot bring himself to walk up to Troy, again sends a message that a heavy rain would ruin the harvest if the ricks were not covered.

Troy ignores the warning and insists that Gabriel is being overanxious. Gabriel starts for home, since he cannot bear watching the scene in the barn. Troy keeps up the celebration and orders a powerful drink of brandy and water for each of the guests. Bathsheba begs him not to give it to the workers, since they are not used to such drinks, and several of the rustics agree, but Troy shrugs off the suggestion and sends the women home so that the men can really enjoy themselves. He threatens to dismiss any man who does not join in the fun.

As Gabriel walks home, he notices signs of the insect and animal life preparing for the storm; the sheep seem terrified and huddle together for protection. Certain that he is right about a bad rain storm, he returns to the stock yard. He resolves that the crop will not be lost and leave his still beloved Bathsheba penniless. He hurries to the barn to get some help to cover the ricks, but all of the men are sleeping off the effects of the strong drinks, and he must save the ricks alone. He manages to find out where he can get the coverings he needs, but he cannot get the key to the granary (storehouse) from Tall. The men are hardly to blame, since they are unused to such drinking and are reduced to this unconscious state in a short time. Gabriel is very worried about the crop and hurries to the village to get the key from Tall's wife. A few minutes later, he begins to drag out four waterproof coverings for two stacks, but there were no more cloths for the three wheat stacks. He decides to slope the sheaves and protect the openings with wheat from some untied sheaves.

After the wheat was safely secured in this way, he starts on the barley, which must be protected by thatching (covering it with straw, leaves, etc.). The moon disappears and the air becomes very still as he frantically keeps up his work.

Comment

It is obvious that Troy is no farmer; he enjoys his power as master of the farm, but cares very little about its practical managing. Since he is so close to the "natural" world, Gabriel is able to assess the strength of the imminent storm; his double devotion to the farm and Bathsheba gives him the conviction that he is right about the storm and eventually helps so save the crops.

CHAPTER XXXVII: THE STORM - THE TWO TOGETHER

Lightning and thunder begin as Gabriel continues and he notices that a candle has been lighted in Bathsheba's window. From his position on top of a stack, Gabriel can see the effect of the lightning on the countryside, and realizes that he is not safe there. He decides to climb down, but since the rain has not yet started, he changes his mind and resolves to finish his task. As a precaution, however, he attaches a chain to his rod (which supported the sheaves as he worked) to act as a ground. When he starts to work again, he is joined by Bathsheba, who has been disturbed by the coming storm and is worried about the harvest.

She asks for Troy and Gabriel tells her he is asleep in the barn; when she offers to help, Gabriel tells her to pass up the sheaves to him, if she is not afraid of climbing the ladder in the dark. The lightning continues, getting brighter with each flash, until it is climaxed by a brilliant flare of light (appearing in the form of dancing skeletons of blue fire) and the rick is struck. The two are saved by Gabriel's "lightning rod," but a tree near-by is destroyed. Realizing their narrow escape, Gabriel tells Bathsheba to go down, but she refuses. The worst part of the storm seems to have passed, and Gabriel says that they are lucky to have been spared a heavy rain.

Bathsheba thanks him for his work in saving the grain and wonders why he has had no help. He tries to defend the others, but she realizes what has happened to them. She follows Gabriel to the barn and sees the men all asleep. When she and Gabriel take up their work again, she questions him on his reaction to her marriage. She tells him that she would die if he thought badly of her and explains that her sudden marriage was forced by circumstances. She thought her reputation would by ruined by her meeting Troy at Bath, and when he told her of another beautiful woman he had seen that day, and that if she didn't marry him soon, he could not promise to be faithful, she married him, torn as she was between jealousy and distraction. She tries to defend Troy, but Gabriel does not answer. Gabriel notices that she is getting tired and tells her he can finish alone. She agrees to go if she cannot be of more help, and worries about his safety. He compliments her on her help and she thanks him for his devotion.

Gabriel quietly finishes his task and thinks about her story; he feels that they are closer now than they had ever been while she was still single. He is disturbed by the sound of the turning of the weather vane; the change of wind indicates a heavy rain.

Comment

The powerful description of the storm is worthy of comparison with the great bonfire scene in Return of the Native. The effect is just as dramatic, but the linking of the fire with the customs, as well as the fate of the characters, is more technically refined in the later novel. Hardy is still developing this technique, but the reader can still be impressed by the vivid imagery.

The chapter also directs the reader's attention to the development of Bathsheba's relationship with Gabriel; she respects his understanding of the operation of the natural, rural world; his perceptive observations and contact with this world have served her well. Troy's hold on her is weakening, as she obviously depends more and more on Gabriel's judgment; her emotional response to Gabriel is deepening, which can be seen by her feeling the need to explain and defend her marriage to him.

CHAPTER XXXVIII: RAIN - ONE SOLITARY MEETS ANOTHER

At dawn, Gabriel is still at his task. He weights down some of the thatching on the wheat and as the rain starts returns to finish protecting the barley. He is immediately drenched in the downpour and as he works, he remembers that it was on this same spot that he had worked to save the stacks from a fire only eight months before. By seven o'clock he is finished; despite his weariness he is satisfied that he saved the crop for the woman he loved. The rustics wake in the barn and start for home; Troy enters the farmhouse, but no one even thinks of the danger of the rain for the harvest.

Gabriel starts home himself and meets Boldwood; Gabriel tells him he looks quite changed, but Boldwood insists that he is perfectly well. Gabriel asks if Boldwood's harvest is safe; he seems distracted, but he finally admits that his own stacks were left uncovered and moreover seems indifferent to their loss. Gabriel realizes how upset Boldwood has been by Bathsheba's marriage; a short time ago it would be unthinkable for Boldwood to appear so bad a farmer. Gabriel tries to console Boldwood but he breaks down and tells Gabriel that he has almost stopped believing in God's mercy. He tries to regain his control as he starts to leave and assures Gabriel that he will soon forget his loss; he asks Gabriel not to mention their meeting and conversation.

Gabriel's familiarity with the ways of nature makes him successful in defying the force of the storm. He does not have to fight nature often; his relationship is based on understanding, and like the oak, he can bend before the wind and not be destroyed.

But Boldwood cannot bend; his spirit is therefore broken by his sense of loss. Gabriel has suffered a disastrous defeat in the loss of his sheep, but was not destroyed by it; he becomes a better man and farmer, despite his loss. Boldwood allows his farm to deteriorate, just as he refuses to be resigned to his fate.

CHAPTER XXXIX: COMING HOME - A CRY

Since the road between Casterbridge and Weatherbury crosses Yalbury Hill, it is customary for farmers and people in light carriages to walk up the hill to ease the horse's burden up the slope. One Saturday evening in October, Bathsheba and Troy are returning from the market and make their way up this hill; Bathsheba is in the carriage guiding the horse, and Troy walks beside her.

Bathsheba seems quite depressed, but Troy is gayer than ever; he excuses his losses by blaming the weather, but Bathsheba reminds him that his losses stem from horse-betting. She asks him to promise to stay away from the next races at Budmouth, but Troy refuses and complains that she has disappointed him by her attitude. As they near the top of the hill, they see a woman walking along the road. Troy is just getting ready to climb into the carriage, when the woman asks if he knows the closing time at the Casterbridge Union (a workhouse).

He seems to recognize her voice, but he carefully controls his reaction as he answers her negatively. The woman seems to recognize him and then faints in the road. Troy orders Bathsheba to go on to the top of the hill and says he will take care of the woman. As Bathsheba moves on, Troy gently questions the woman about where she has been and what she is doing at Weatherbury now. She tells him that she has been afraid to write and admits that she has no money. Troy tells her that he cannot help her now; he regrets her having to go to the Union, but he tells her that he will meet her Monday morning and bring her some money. He promises the woman - finally identified as Fanny Robin - that he will take care of her and that he regrets abandoning her.

As she reaches the top of the hill, Bathsheba turns to see Troy hurrying to join her and the woman slowly continuing her way toward Casterbridge. Troy silently takes up the reins and Bathsheba asks if he knows the woman. Troy admits he does, but not by name, and refuses to explain any further.

Comment

The rift between Bathsheba and Troy is rapidly widening; the marriage that was based on such shaky foundations is obviously being slowly destroyed. Their separation is subtly hinted at by the picture of Bathsheba riding alone in the carriage, as Troy walks.

The mysterious woman that the two pass on the road is obviously Fanny, as the reader quickly guesses; Hardy is making use of the "veiled woman" technique in hiding her identity for effect. He hints at Fanny's plight after Troy's desertion by having her inquire about the workhouse, the last resort for the poverty-stricken at that time. Troy realizes he must help Fanny, but typically delays meeting her until the postponement becomes the margin between life and death for Fanny.

CHAPTER XL: ON CASTERBRIDGE HIGHWAY

For some time Fanny continues walking, becoming weaker with each step, until she sinks down by a haystack and falls asleep. When she awakes, night has fallen and she can dimly see the lights of Casterbridge in the distance. She gathers up all her strength to walk the remaining few miles, reminding herself that she is to meet Troy on Monday, but realizes that she might well be in her grave by then.

She hears one o'clock strike as she continues her journey; the light from a passing carriage shows her young face marred by much suffering. As she passes the two-mile mark, she takes courage at the short distance left, but her ebbing strength causes her to stop to pick up two branches for crutches. With this help, she manages to pass the one-mile mark, but her exhaustion finally causes her to faint. After a few minutes, she pulls herself up, and with the aid of her sticks, continues bravely on. She painfully creeps onward, counting guideposts to shorten the journey. When she crawls on to the bridge between the highway and Casterbridge, she comforts herself by the thought that she has only a half mile left; but she is too tired to continue.

She lies down on the bridge and tries to think of some way to continue. A large dog comes by and licks her cheek; she struggles up and, leaning on the dog for support, manages to start on her journey again. When she can, she cheerfully urges the dog onward; she carefully avoids any human help and seems anxious not to be recognized.

Despite her slow progress, she finally reaches the Casterbridge Union. She has just about enough strength left to reach the bell pull before she faints on the door step. By now, it is six o'clock in the morning and some of the people inside are moving about. A man opens the door and helps her in; she asks about the dog outside, but he tells her that he threw stones at it and chased it away. The man walks ahead, carrying a light, while two women support Fanny and take her further into the building.

Comment

Fanny's journey to Casterbridge is surely one of the most agonizing miniature odysseys produced in literature. Hardy wrings out every emotional response possible to gain sympathy for Fanny; in fact, her using the dog as a support is melodramatic and borders on the ridiculous (reminiscent of Liza's jumping over the ice floes in Harriet Beecher Stowe's *Uncle Tom's Cabin*). It is ironic that she is helped on her way only by the dog; humanity (especially Troy) seems to have deserted her. Of course, she is accepted at the workhouse, but the callousness of the personnel is evidenced by the man's driving away the dog by throwing stones.

Fanny's obvious desire to keep from being recognized arouses the reader's curiosity; it seems that there is something more than her lack of money that Fanny is hiding from Troy.

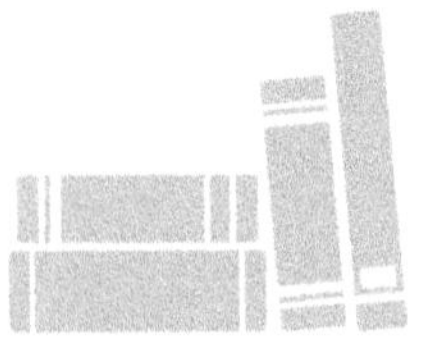

FAR FROM THE MADDING CROWD

TEXTUAL ANALYSIS

CHAPTERS 41-49

CHAPTER XLI: SUSPICION - FANNY IS SENT FOR

The evening after the meeting with Fanny and most of the next day, is spent silently and painfully by Bathsheba and Troy. Troy finally asks her for twenty pounds, telling her that it was for the races. Bathsheba begs him not to go; Troy refuses to stay home and insists on the money, admitting he needs it, but not for the races. She promises him some money from her household funds, but she regrets the conflicts that are running their marriage. She feels that he is ignoring her, as he would never have in the past.

Troy insists he must go away on the next day, and, taking out his watch, opens the back of the case to stare at the lock of hair which it encloses. Bathsheba accidentally looks up and notices the hair; she is very distressed and cries out, asking whose hair it is. Troy, assuming a casual air, tells her it is hers and that he had almost forgotten he had it. Bathsheba knows he is lying, since the hair is blond, and again questions him about it. Troy arouses her jealousy by admitting that it belongs to a pretty young woman, who is still unmarried.

The argument continues until Bathsheba asks Troy to burn the hair, but Troy is too angry to make peace and tells her he regrets their marriage as much as she does. Bathsheba is a bit frightened by his words and insists that she regrets marrying him only if he loves someone else. Troy lets slip that his meeting with the woman on the road reminded him of his past ties. Bathsheba desperately begs him to tell her the truth about the woman and she humbles herself to ask for justice. Her pride is conquered; she laments her infatuation for Troy, since it had brought her unhappiness and humiliation.

When she returns from her customary ride around the farm the next morning, she is told that Troy has left for Casterbridge. She regains some of her poise by the end of breakfast and sets off to walk to another section of the farm. She allows herself to think of Gabriel's devotion and wonders what marriage to him would be like. As she walks along, she sees Boldwood meet with Oak and talk for a few minutes; the two call to Poorgrass, as he is passing by. When Boldwood leaves, she asks Joseph what has happened and he tells her that Fanny Robin has died at the Casterbridge Union. He is not certain of the facts about her death, but does tell her that Boldwood plans to send a wagon to bring the body back to Weatherbury for burial.

Bathsheba sincerely pities the girl and, since she was once part of Bathsheba's uncle's household, orders Joseph to prepare a new wagon and to place evergreen and flowers in it to cover Fanny's coffin; she accepts the responsibility for Fanny's burial herself. Joseph tells her that Fanny had been at the Union only a few days; she was supposed to have lived in a garrison-town and then as a seamstress before he return. Bathsheba immediately realizes that Fanny is the woman she and Troy had passed on the road. She nearly faints, but controls herself enough to ask Joseph the color of Fanny's hair; but he does not remember.

About an hour later, Joseph brings the wagon to her for inspection. She is still upset and asks if Joseph has learned anything more about Fanny. He only knows what Boldwood and Gabriel have told him, however, and she sends him on his sad journey.

After he leaves, Bathsheba questions Liddy about Fanny and discovers that she had beautiful blond hair, and that her sweetheart was a soldier in Troy's regiment. Liddy adds that Troy once told her that he knew Fanny's young man very well and that, in fact, they looked very much alike. The report is too much for Bathsheba to bear, and she nervously stops Liddy's gossiping.

Comment

The title of the chapter certainly misleads the reader; Fanny is hardly expected to be sent for in this manner. It is the dead Fanny, however, that proves a more successful rival to Bathsheba than Fanny alive could ever have been. Her shadow has been a third party to the marriage from the beginning, but a shadow Bathsheba could defy. It seems ironic that the weak and defenseless Fanny is the one who innocently forces the final wedge into the crack that has been widening in the marriage.

Troy's postponement of help for Fanny has had tragic results; she tragically disappoints him again at this meeting but his realization and remorse is yet to come. Bathsheba's manner in reacting to Fanny's needs is far more charitable than Troy's; she acts immediately and accepts responsibility for the burial. It is unfortunate that her charity is repaid by the recognition of the depth of Troy's involvement with Fanny.

CHAPTER XLII: JOSEPH AND HIS BURDEN - BUCK'S HEAD

A wall surrounds the Casterbridge Union, and only an oddly-placed door breaks its surface. The bottom of the door was a few feet off the ground; although it was meant to be used for loading and unloading wagons, the grass growing around it showed it was not often opened. Poorgrass is sent to this door, and a plain coffin is brought out and placed in the wagon by two men. One of them writes on the coffin-lid with some chalk, and then the coffin is covered by a black cloth. Joseph is given a registration certificate; he covers the coffin with the flowers and greens, as he has been directed. As he starts back to Weatherbury, he is caught in a dense fog; he regrets his lonesome trip, and, as he approaches Buck's Head Inn, he decides to get a mug of ale to cheer him on his way. Unfortunately for Fanny, and the plan to have her buried by closing time at the Weatherbury churchyard, Poorgrass meets Clark and Coggan, who urge him to keep drinking to make up for being out on such a wretched day.

Although Poorgrass explains his errand, his two friends keep ordering round after round of ale; the longer he stays, the less importance Joseph gives to his task. Gabriel appears, angry at Joseph for his neglect; the two friends try to excuse Joseph, and Gabriel realizes that by now Poorgrass is in no condition to continue. Gabriel leaves and drives the wagon to Weatherbury himself. He meets the parson who tells him that it is now too late for the burial, and since Poorgrass still has the registration certificate, it would be better to put off the funeral until the next day. He suggests bringing the body to the church for the night; Gabriel agrees that this plan seems best, but the decision must be Bathsheba's.

At first she seems to think that the church would be the best place for the body back to remain during the night, but, realizing that the farm was the only home Fanny had known for years, she feels that it would only be charitable to bring the body to the farm. The parson agrees that Bathsheba is right. The coffin is brought into a little sitting room and placed on two benches. Gabriel remains alone with the coffin for a little while; he is deeply troubled at the outcome of events. In spite of all he has done to spare Bathsheba's feelings, she must suffer the awkwardness of having the body of her rival brought to her own home. He thinks of the agony she will feel at the terrible discovery of Fanny's secret. In a last effort to spare Bathsheba this sad news too soon, he erases the last two words from the chalk inscription on the coffin. The message had read "Fanny Robin and child," but now only her name is left on the coffin as Gabriel quietly leaves the house.

Comment

Again the cold indifference of institutions is suggested by the callous transferal of Fanny's body to the wagon. In a very efficient manner, responsibility for Fanny is discharged; the damaging inscription is written and the certificate changes hands briskly and without further thought. Even after death, an unhappy fate strikes; the least dependable worker is sent for Fanny who suffers a final indignity as the wagon patiently waits outside Buck's Head Inn.

The **climax** of the chapter is most effective; Hardy so structures the developments that the reader's attention is riveted on the coffin and its inscription. Both Fanny's reputation and Bathsheba's peace of mind seem to be saved by Gabriel's kind gesture, but mistakes and their consequences cannot be so easily erased.

CHAPTER XLIII: FANNY'S REVENGE

Late that evening Liddy talks briefly with Bathsheba and offers to sit up to wait for Troy. Bathsheba sends her to bed and prepares to wait by the one lighted fire. She feels her new loneliness and pain acutely. She wonders what effect this tragedy will have on her marriage; Liddy returns to bring some news of Fanny and whispers it in Bathsheba's ear. Bathsheba insists that only one name is on the coffin lid, but she is so upset by the possibility that Fanny's child is buried with her that sleep is impossible. She is not sophisticated enough to ignore its importance and grows more and more miserable in thinking of Fanny's fate and her own unhappiness. Had Gabriel only realized how much indecision and suspense his simple erasure had caused, he could never have brought himself to cause such agony.

Bathsheba decides to ask Gabriel to tell her what he knows; she hurries out to his cottage, but when she sees him saying his night prayers and closing out his lights, she determines to find out the truth for herself. She returns to the house and frantically searches for a screwdriver; she opens the coffin, and, as she looks at the enclosed bodies, tells herself that it is best to know the worst. She thinks that such an invasion of privacy would have once seemed terrible, but now it seems trivial in comparison to Troy's shameful desertion of Fanny. She weeps over the two bodies and realizes that Fanny has triumphed over her, by her death. The dead Fanny excites only pity and not jealousy or revenge. She kneels by the opened coffin to pray and rises with a quieted soul. She moves about the coffin and lays flowers around Fanny's head; her distracted actions are interrupted by Troy's return.

Slowly he begins to understand the meaning of the scene, but he does not yet connect Fanny with the corpse. Bathsheba tries to leave but Troy asks her who had died and pulls her back to the coffin. The candlelight reveals the dead mother and child; Troy is shocked by the full realization of Fanny's plight. Bathsheba asks if he knows the girl and he admits it; she has never suffered as she does now, watching his reaction to the sight before him. He bends over and kisses Fanny; Bathsheba cannot bear the pain and begs him not to kiss Fanny and her child, but if he must, to kiss her too, since she loves him more than Fanny ever did.

Troy looks at her as if he does not recognize her; he pushes her away and finally tells her that he has been wicked and that Fanny is his victim. He cruelly insists that he had loved Fanny and that she had meant more to him than anyone else ever can. He had only become infatuated with Bathsheba and he should have married Fanny; the crowning blow is his statement that in the sight of heaven Fanny is his true wife. He is not morally Bathsheba's, despite their marriage; Bathsheba feels a wild impulse to run from him and hide. She rushes out of the door into the dark.

Comment

Although the reader is tempted to forgive Troy by virtue of his search for Fanny and the realization that he does not know about the child until now, Troy's cruel treatment of Bathsheba, his recognition of Fanny on the road and his postponement of immediate aid, and most especially, his refusal to marry Fanny earlier, simply because she embarrassed him when she failed to meet him at the church, make such forgiveness impossible.

Boldwood's curse has finally touched Troy; at no other point in the story is Troy as miserable and unhappy. He misses the last opportunity to re-establish his relationship with Bathsheba when he coldly ignores her as he finally identifies himself with Fanny. Just as he once treated Fanny indifferently, he fails to sympathize with the effect that this development has on Bathsheba. He can help Bathsheba; Fanny is beyond needing his help. It is perhaps Troy's fatal flaw that he is always too late-or in the wrong place-to understand or to help anyone.

CHAPTER XLIV: UNDER A TREE - REACTION

Bathsheba runs out along the dark road until she finds a ferncovered shelter and falls down there to sleep at last. She is awakened by the early morning sounds: birds chirping and a singing ploughboy walking to work. She watches the sunrise and stares at the beauty of the dawn on the land around her. She is amused at hearing a schoolboy reciting his lesson as he passes, and suddenly she sees Liddy, who has come out to search for her. Liddy reports that Troy has left early that morning and Fanny's body has not yet been taken away for burial.

Bathsheba decides not to return just yet; Liddy brings her a small breakfast and a warm wrap. Since Fanny's body is still at the house, the two stroll about the woods until Liddy is sent back to see if Bathsheba can return. Liddy tells the workers that Bathsheba is in her room and is not to be disturbed.

Bathsheba decides to remain and accept her troubles; she refuses to tell Liddy what dreadful tragedy has torn her marriage apart. They return to the house and Bathsheba hides in an unused attic. She passes the day reading light literature, but the precaution of hiding from Troy is not necessary for he does not return all day. As the sun begins to set, Bathsheba watches the village boys playing, but the game ends abruptly. The next time Liddy comes up to the room, Bathsheba inquires about the sudden finish; Liddy tells her that a carved tombstone has just arrived from Casterbridge and the boys probably went to see whose it was. Liddy adds that she knows nothing more about it.

Comment

The night of betrayal gives way to a dawn of serenity. Bathsheba wakes to the dawn of a new day, and the dawn of a new maturity. But this maturity is only incipient as she reverts to the childish act of hiding in the attic to avoid facing Troy.

Again Hardy piques the reader's curiosity when he introduces the tombstone at the end of the chapter. The reader can guess it is for Fanny, but we must wait for the next chapter to discover who ordered t and how the monument arrived at Weatherbury so quickly after Fanny's burial.

CHAPTER XLV: TROY'S ROMANTICISM

After Bathsheba had left the house, Troy covered the dead bodies and then went upstairs to wait for morning. He had waited for Fanny at the appointed place and grew angry as she disappointed him for the second time. He rides off to the races at Budmouth, but he cannot bring himself to bet any money. He stays until about nine o'clock and then rides home slowly; he begins to realize that perhaps illness had detained Fanny and regrets not asking about her at Casterbridge. On his return, he makes his tragic discovery.

As soon as it starts to get light, Troy leaves the house without a thought about Bathsheba. He locates Fanny's newly dug grave in the churchyard and then hurries to Casterbridge. He finds a stone mason and orders an elaborate tombstone; he places his order as simply as a child might. He asks for the best possible memorial he can get for twenty-seven pounds, all the money he had (that was to be Fanny's). He writes out the inscription he wants placed on the stone, waits in town until the stone is ready, and watches it placed in a cart for transport to Weatherbury.

Carrying a heavy basket on his arm, he leaves Casterbridge when it is dark. He meets the cart returning from Weatherbury and is satisfied to hear that the tombstone has been erected. Although it is now about ten o'clock, he searches for Fanny's grave in the dark, gets a spade and lantern, and, by its light, plants the flowers he has brought in his basket. Carefully, he lays out the plants and arranges them with attention. He does not feel foolish at his romantic action, but works through the dark night until it begins to rain. Since he is tired and the rain seems to get heavier, he decides to finish the work in the morning and falls asleep on a bench placed in the porch of the church.

Comment

Hardy's grim humor is evident in Troy's use of the money he planned to give Fanny to buy her an elaborate tombstone. It is additionally ironic that the man who denied Fanny in life should so dramatically accept identification with her after her death. The gesture of his ordering a large marble stone recalls the impulsive gift of the valuable watch to Bathsheba. Even in repentance, Troy must be melodramatic. However genuine Troy's grief and self-recrimination, the reader is always aware that these tender gestures to Fanny are too late; Troy's planting of the flowers suggests a romantic and impractical nature, but it cannot excuse his earlier desertion of Fanny and his cruel rejection of Bathsheba.

CHAPTER XLVI: THE GURGOYLE: ITS DOINGS

Fanny's grave was in the churchyard of Weatherbury Church, erected in the fourteenth century, square in shape, and ornamented by two stone gargoyles (gurgoyles) on each of the corners of the square. These gargoyles had been built not only for ornament, but to allow the rain to run off the lead roof. Water gushed through the wide-open mouths of the sometimes hideous faces of the gargoyles; each one was carved differently from the other, a lack of symmetry associated with the Gothic art of the continent. The passing of time and the decision of the churchwardens had put all but two of these water-spouts out of use.

While Troy slept, the rain kept on; soon water began falling from one of the two functionary gargoyles. The heavy rain caused a small stream to pour from the wall and over towards Fanny's grave. The stones that had been arranged to protect the soil from such a deluge had been dislodged by the force of the falling water. Since the corner in which Fanny's grave was located was not very often used, or visited, no one was aware of the danger to the graves from the rain.

The pouring water rushes into the loose soil of Fanny's grave and soon a pool of water is formed. The flowers that Troy had so carefully planted are loosened and destroyed; some plants actually float away.

Troy's two rather sleepless nights cause him to sleep until broad daylight; he awakes to find the landscape presenting a bright new prospect. As he walks towards Fanny's grave, he notices that the path is covered with mud and sees some of the flowers he had planted moved quite a distance by the flood. The water has hollowed the earth over the grave; the displaced earth has become mud that spots even the new tombstone. Nearly all of the flowers are washed away.

The sight upsets Troy more than ever; the flooding seems to be the last blow of Fate. It seems to **climax** the tragedy he discovered so shortly before, and it is more than he can bear. For the first time in his life, Troy hates himself; he is thoroughly miserable and feels himself especially marked for disaster. He leaves the grave, not even bothering to fill the hollow or to re-arrange the flowers; he seems to give up decisive action completely, and leaves the village.

Bathsheba has noticed the lantern light in the churchyard from her attic window. At dawn, she opens the window to the fresh new day; Liddy brings her some breakfast and tells her that Gabriel has gone to investigate the strange noise coming from one of the spouts on the church roof. Bathsheba asks if there is any news of Troy; Liddy tells her that he has been seen on the road to Budmouth.

Bathsheba walks to the churchyard and locates the ruined grave; she and Gabriel stare at the elaborate stone. She sadly reads the inscription, "Erected by Francis Troy in Beloved Memory of Fanny Robin."

She directs Gabriel to fill in the hollow of the grave while she collects the displaced flowers and re-plants them. She asks Gabriel to get the churchwardens to turn the leadwork at the mouth of the spout to prevent another such flooding. Her suffering has refined her instinctive reactions; very charitably, she wipes the mudstains from the stone, as if she really appreciated the sentiment expressed by the inscription.

Comment

Fortune seems totally against Troy at this point; everything he touches is ruined. His last attempt to repair his injury to Fanny is thwarted by a natural force, rain. Troy has never been as conscious of nature as Gabriel is, and is hardly sympathetic to the "natural" world, which seems to be paying him back for his neglect. The flowers he plant are washed away; he abandons them, and Weatherbury.

Troy has learned little from his suffering and he acts childishly in simply leaving his troubles behind as he leaves town. He coldly abandons Bathsheba to face the embarrassment of the inscription on the stone; her charity and serene acceptance of suffering is disclosed by her cleaning the tombstone and re-arranging the flowers.

CHAPTER XLVII: ADVENTURES BY THE SHORE

Troy, terribly distracted by the sad events of the past few days and reluctant to return home to Bathsheba, wanders along the road to the south. By the middle of the afternoon, he finds himself near a slope that runs to the top of a group of hills which separate the valley of cultivated land from the coast. As he nears the top of this road, he sees the broad sea before him, and, on his right, the town of Budmouth. The area seems totally deserted; nothing seems to move except the lapping waves at the sea shore. He discovers a small cover and decides to rest here and take a swim before walking on. The cove is surrounded by cliffs, except for one section which opens out to the sea; Troy leaves his clothes at the water's edge and swims out to sea. As he swims, he recalls hearing that in this area many swimmers have been drowned because of the current. No boat is in sight as Troy desperately tries to get back to the cove; he swims on, trying to conserve his strength. As he moves further towards the right, he sees a ship's boat and swims toward it. The sailors hear his shouts and row in his direction; a few minutes later, Troy is pulled into the boat. The sailors had come ashore for sand; they lend him what clothes they can and agree to put him ashore in the morning. As it grows dark, they row quickly to their ship. The only sound to be heard is that of their oars; the only sight, for miles, is that of the ship toward which they move.

Comment

Troy's amazing luck has not completely deserted him. His rescue may seem badly contrived, but Troy's mysterious disappearance and the expectation of his return later on in the story, helps to maintain the reader's interest.

The device used in introducing the sailors as Troy's saviors is termed **deus ex machina**. A force totally out of the story intervenes to save him; the sailors and ship appear only when they are needed and are out of the main thread of the story: for it would be difficult to explain why some familiar character should keep Troy's rescue a secret. Hardy was thus forced to fall back on this contrivance to remove Troy temporarily from the scene, but yet to keep the expectation of his return very much alive.

CHAPTER XLVIII: DOUBTS ARISE - DOUBTS LINGER

Bathsheba accepts her husband's absence with surprise and some relief; she seems indifferent about his return. The newly humbled young woman weighs the outcome of his return; she might have to leave Weatherbury Farm. She knows that if she (or Troy) fails to pay the rent due in January, very little consideration would be given her (since there had been some objection to her inheriting the farm) and she would again be reduced to poverty. She feels sure that her marriage had been a mistake; calmly she awaits the outcome.

The first Saturday after Troy's disappearance, she went to Casterbridge to the market; she notices a man who had been looking for her and hears him speak to someone near-by. He asks for Mrs. Troy and is told that she is standing close to them; Bathsheba's sensitive hearing catches the rest of the news: Troy has been drowned. She is shocked by the news and cannot believe it; her self-command gives way and she faints. Boldwood catches her in his arms and asks what the news is. He is told that Troy was drowned near Lulwind Cove; Troy's clothes were found and brought into Budmouth the day before. Boldwood carries Bathsheba to a private room to give her time to recover; she regains consciousness and asks to return home.

Boldwood leaves the room delighted that for a few minutes Bathsheba had been in his arms; he sends a woman in to take care of her and goes out to see if he can find out more about the disaster. Boldwood offers to get someone to drive Bathsheba home, or to drive her home himself, but she refuses and, when she feels a bit more controlled, starts to drive home alone. When she returns, she goes upstairs at once; the news had already reached Weatherbury, but no one disturbs her as she goes up to her room and sits quietly by the window until quite dark. To Liddy's question if she would like to order some mourning clothes, Bathsheba says no, for she is sure Troy is still alive. She remains firm in this conviction until the evidence gathered during the next few days seems to confirm his death, even though the body has not been found.

When Troy's clothes are returned, she realizes that he had planned to come back to shore and dress again; nothing but death would have prevented him from returning. She wonders if Troy had been so distressed by Fanny's death that he schemed to make a suicide look like an accident, but she was not blind to the possibility that Troy's death might mean something worse, such as a rejection of her. Late that evening, she examines the lock of hair still enclosed in Troy's watch; she realizes that the two belonged together in life, and perhaps they were together again in death. At first she thinks she should burn the hair, but finally decides to keep it, in memory of Fanny.

Comment

Troy's impulsive action has again caused pain that he had never considered would result; he thinks only of himself and his own troubles, coldly ignoring the effect his disappearance will have on Bathsheba and her obvious need for him at this time.

Bathsheba, on the other hand, has developed far from the thoughtless girl first introduced to the reader; her concern for others is obvious in her reaction to the news of Troy, and her acceptance of his bond with Fanny.

CHAPTER XLIX: OAK'S ADVANCEMENT - A GREAT HOPE

As autumn starts to give way to winter, Bathsheba is living quietly, if not peacefully, regretting her past mistakes. She manages the farm without too much interest; Gabriel, however, is finally appointed bailiff officially, although he served in that capacity for a long time without the title.

Boldwood's farm is far from prosperous; he lives alone and is so preoccupied with his troubles that he neglects his crops. Repeatedly his workers remind him of his duties, but he ignores the warning until the farm is ruined. He sends for Gabriel finally and asks him to become supervisor of the farm without abandoning his duties at Bathsheba's farm. Gabriel's fortune, at least, seems to be getting better; Bathsheba first objects to Gabriel's double chores, but finally agrees, since the farms are situated next to each other.

Gabriel's prosperity is noted by the villagers; Susan Tall, for one, comments on his improved appearance. His agreement with Boldwood, which allows him a share of the profits instead of a fixed wage, makes Gabriel modestly well off financially; since he continues to live as simply as before, some villagers consider him miserly, but Gabriel is only holding on to old habits.

Boldwood, still determined to win Bathsheba despite all his past unhappiness, is seized by the great hope that she will agree to marry him at last. She is no longer the vain young woman who toyed with his love; in fact, her troubles seem to have made her beauty and charm more desirable than ever.

When Bathsheba returns from a two months' visit to her aunt at Norcombe, Boldwood takes the opportunity to ask Liddy about her. He flatters the girl about her close connection with

Bathsheba and Liddy confides that if Bathsheba should marry again they would still remain together. Boldwood grasps the slight hope this hint seems to offer and asks about Bathsheba's plans for marriage. Liddy insists that Bathsheba never talks of marriage, but that she once said she might marry at the end of seven years (the legal period necessary to declare Troy dead). Boldwood insists that no such waiting period is necessary; Liddy asks if he has discussed the matter with some lawyers. He denies this and hurries away; he is quite angry with himself for appearing so foolish and underhanded, but at least he has found out something of value. Six more years was indeed a long time, but his eventual reward was worth it. He would patiently wait out that time, and prove how little the delay would affect his devotion.

Meanwhile, that summer the Greenhill Fair was held, which was frequently attended by the people of Weatherbury.

Comment

Boldwood, unlike Gabriel, has not learned to accept his fate philosophically; he continues to yearn for Bathsheba, despite all his previous disappointments. This insistence on winning Bathsheba has become almost a mad obsession, and it will destroy him if he cannot learn to control it.

Gabriel, on the other hand, remains patient and tolerant; he still is devoted to Bathsheba, but he has learned to live with his pain. He has never acted contrary to nature. He has suffered most of his trials through no fault of his own, and now seems to be rewarded by good fortune.

FAR FROM THE MADDING CROWD

TEXTUAL ANALYSIS

CHAPTERS 50–57

CHAPTER L: THE SHEEP FAIR - TROY TOUCHES HIS WIFE'S HAND

The Greenhill Fair, visited by people from all of South Wessex, was extremely popular. The busiest day of the fair was that of the sheep sales; the sheep were penned on the top of a hill which was surrounded by the ruins of an ancient earthwork (a man-built mound). Shepherds brought their flocks from distances, travelling ten or twelve miles a day and resting for the night in hired fields by the side of the road. Special provisions were made for sheep that became lame, or simply worn out, and for lambs that were born during the trip. Weatherbury Farms were not too far from the fair, but Gabriel had to supervise both flocks; the large united flock needed the additional attention of Boldwood's shepherd, Cainy, and George, Gabriel's old dog.

At another section of the hill, a large tent was erected and a special theatrical performance was announced, "The Royal

Hippodrome Performance of Turpin's Ride to York and the Death of Black Bess." As the flocks were sold and owners and shepherds shed their responsibilities, many of them made their way to this tent. Squeezed in among the crowd waiting for admission were Coggan and Poorgrass, who were at the fair for a holiday. The two finally enter the tent, which has a section reserved in the rear for dressing rooms. In the area set apart for the male performers, a young man sits on the grass pulling on boots; he is recognized as Sergeant Troy.

Troy's history since his disappearance from Weatherbury is summarized. Because the ship to which Troy's rescuers were rowing was short of crewmembers, Troy signed on as a seaman, but when his clothes were sent for their loss was discovered. He worked his passage to the United States and made a scanty living giving lessons in gymnastics (including sword handling, fencing and boxing). When he tired of this life, he decided to return to England and claim a more secure life at Weatherbury Farm. He wondered if Bathsheba considered him as living or as dead; in any case, he determined to regain his former position. By the time he reached Liverpool, however, he began to worry about his reception and Bathsheba's attitude toward him. In addition, he thinks that she might-well have lost the farm by now and then he would be responsible for taking care of her; this prospect, especially with the memory of Fanny haunting them both, made the thought of his quick return home rather unpleasant. He delayed his return trip and took any type of work he could find; finally, he joined a travelling circus and, by using his skill as a marksman, became a member of the troupe. His talents were recognized and the play about Turpin was prepared largely for him to display his talents as the hero. Troy thought of this position as only temporary, and since he was indifferent to where the company performed, found himself at Greenhill, not far from Weatherbury.

As the sun began to set and the time of the performance approached, Bathsheba arrived at the tent; she was as curious as anyone about the performance, and was eager to see it. She meets Boldwood, who asks if her sheep had sold for a good price. She tells him that the sheep were sold as soon as they reached the fair, and she has some spare time. She still has one dealer to see and is passing the time away before her appointment by watching the play. She asks if Boldwood knows anything about Turpin; Boldwood admits that he knows little about him, except that one of Coggan's relations was supposed to know a friend of Turpin's.

The performance begins and Boldwood apologizes for keeping her and offers to get her ticket. When he sees Bathsheba's hesitation, he quickly adds that he is on his way home; Bathsheba is eager to see the play, and, since Gabriel is nowhere around, asks Boldwood to act in his place and find a seat for her. He arranges for her seat and leaves; unfortunately, the seat he selected was conspicuous (no one else was in the "reserved" section) and Bathsheba becomes the object of everyone's attention until the play begins. She tries to make the best of the situation and, as she looks over the crowd, is glad to see Coggan and Poorgrass among the spectators.

In this golden haze of the late afternoon sun, Troy peeps from behind the scenes and sees Bathsheba. Although his disguise for the performance would hide his face, he is afraid she will recognize his voice. He debated about going through with his performance; his indifference to his reception at Weatherbury had changed, partly by his shame at her finding him in so low an occupation, and partly because she had never appeared so beautiful. Troy's wits were sharpened by challenges such as this; he immediately tells the manager that a creditor who might recognize him is present and asks if his part might be played silently. The manager agrees and adds that the spectators would probably not realize that Troy's speeches had been omitted, since much of the play's impact depended on action and not dialogue. The audience is very pleased by the performance; Poorgrass and Coggan are very impressed, and Poorgrass is especially thrilled when he joins the volunteers to carry out Bess at the end of the play - an experience he can describe with pride for years to come.

Troy had taken extra pains with his make-up and managed to get through the performance undetected. During the next performance, however, his luck runs out: he is recognized by Pennyways (the dismissed bailiff who has become Bathsheba's enemy). Troy decides to ignore him, but he starts to worry about the news of his return being spread about Weatherbury. He is anxious to find out about Bathsheba's financial situation before he makes his identity known, so Pennyways must be silenced.

As it gets dark, Troy dons a false beard and searches for Pennyways at the largest refreshment booth at the fair. This booth had been comfortably arranged with a first and second class section, and as fully equipped as any local inn. As Troy enters, he cannot find Pennyways, but sees Bathsheba at the further end seated near the canvas wall of the tent. He hurries around the outside of the tent to where Bathsheba is seated with Boldwood; he hears her voice and quietly cuts the canvas so he can see them as well as overhear her conversation. Bathsheba explains that the buyer she was waiting for has not kept his appointment. Pennyways appears and tells her he has some private information for her. She refuses to listen to him and Pennyways writes this message: "Your husband is here. I've seen him. Who's the fool now?" He folds up the note and, when she will not accept it, tosses it into her lap and leaves.

Although Troy could not see what was written, he guesses that it refers to him; he curses his luck as Boldwood picks up the note to hand it to Bathsheba. Bathsheba transfers the note from her right to her left hand (the hand nearest Troy); he reaches under the tentcloth and, with lightning speed, snatches the note and runs away. He hurries back to the front of the tent to find Pennyways and hears some men talking about the daring attempt to rob a young lady; he then discovers Pennyways standing behind some dancers, and draws him away from the tent with a few whispered words.

Comment

The chapter contains several rapidly developing events. The plot is complicated by the discovery of Troy's return; he controls the outcome of the story from this point on.

Troy's unpleasant traits are at their most obvious in this chapter. He fails to be concerned with Bathsheba's financial and emotional state; he allows her to suffer by not relieving her mind about his safety. His reasons for returning are basically selfish; first he considers his own security by planning to resume his control of the farm, and then he is drawn to Bathsheba because of her charm and beauty that is legally his, by right of their marriage. Considering his state of mind after Fanny's death, his callousness might be forgiven, but one can hardly forgive his hiding his identity he is sure that Bathsheba still owns a prosperous farm.

CHAPTER LI: BATHSHEBA TALKS WITH HER OUTRIDER

Since Poorgrass' visits to the refreshment booth make it impossible for him to drive Bathsheba back to the farm, and

Gabriel must still arrange for the sale of Boldwood's remaining flocks, Bathsheba decides to accept Boldwood's offer to escort her home. She would have preferred Gabriel, but the "robbery" at the tent has frightened her enough to be glad of even Boldwood's company. Furthermore, she feels that it would be unkind to refuse Boldwood, whose devotion is still quite evident.

Boldwood rides his horse close to her carriage; they chatter about the fair and farming, until Boldwood abruptly asks Bathsheba if she would remarry someday. She is confused by the suddenness of the question, and manages to reply that she has not thought seriously about it and that her husband's death has never been absolutely proved.

Boldwood tells her that he regrets having lost her and asks how she feels now about him; he urges her to marry him and repair the injury caused him, if evidence is found that Troy is really dead. She refuses to discuss the possibility, since any remarriage would have to wait until the legal period for declaring Troy dead is over. Boldwood pleads with her to accept him; Bathsheba finally agrees that on Christmas she will promise to marry him at the end of the seven years, If Troy does not return.

Comment

Bathsheba promises Boldwood what he so earnestly desires out of compassion and a sense of justice. She realizes that her foolish joke caused him much anguish, and it is only fair that she pay the penalty for her "crime" by marrying him, even if she does not love him. Bathsheba has been so unhappy in her marriage to Troy that she feels happiness does not exist for her and that she may as well make Boldwood happy in payment for his long devotion and many troubles.

CHAPTER LII: CONVINCING COURSES

This chapter is divided into separate sections.

(1)

At Little Weatherbury Farm, Boldwood prepares an elaborate Christmas party, much to the surprise of his neighbors. The preparations indicate that the party will be especially merry; the house is well decorated for Christmas, and the kitchen fire continues all day long to provide enough food. Floor space for dancing is cleared and two men bring a large log for the fire to warm the guests in the long hall. Something seems to be missing, however, for the host (a usually lonely man not given much to entertaining) leaves the organization of the party to others, and the invited guests feel that a party at this home seems almost unnatural.

(2)

Bathsheba dresses for the dance and tells Liddy that she's sorry she has to attend, since she promised to see Boldwood "on business" at Christmastime. She is nervous and upset because she realizes that she is probably the cause of the party; in frustration she wishes she had never seen Weatherbury. She insists on wearing her black mourning clothes in order to appear as usual and to reflect her reluctance to attend the party.

Bathsheba feels that a stronger will than hers has forced her into her promise and to making her feel that she must promise to marry Boldwood. As Christmas neared, she grew more and more anxious and puzzled about her predicament. One day she meets Gabriel accidentally and tells him about her trouble; Oak reminds her that Boldwood will never forget her. Bathsheba agrees and tells him that she felt that if she did not make this promise Boldwood would go mad. His whole life and well-being seem to depend on her.

Gabriel tells her that the marriage would not be wrong, but he adds that he thinks it sinful of her to marry Boldwood without loving him. Bathsheba, however, tells him that she must pay the price for her cruel joke; she accepts the responsibility and views the marriage as a sort of penance. She refuses to accept any outsider's opinion on love, although she might accept it on other matters, and leaves Gabriel.

She had spoken frankly to Gabriel and did not expect him to react in any other way than the way he did; yet, she feels a bit disappointed that Gabriel did not wish her to marry him. While she did not consider marriage to Gabriel a possibility, she still wishes that he might have mentioned his love for her and is a bit annoyed that he offered his advice so dispassionately.

(3)

At Weatherbury Farm, Boldwood dresses himself more carefully than he has ever done in his life. A tailor from Casterbridge had come to help him try on a new coat, and never had Boldwood been so difficult to please. When he finally seems satisfied, Gabriel comes in to report on the day's progress and Boldwood tells him to make merry that night. He confides his great hope to Gabriel and tells him he worries that something might yet happen to take this joy away. He asks Gabriel's advice on trivial things such as the knot in his tie, and then he questions Gabriel about depending on women to keep their promises.

Gabriel comforts him by replying that a woman may keep a promise if it will repair an injury. Boldwood tells him that he has not yet won an absolute promise, but he is sure that she will agree to an engagement that very night. When Gabriel reminds him that the marriage must wait seven years, Boldwood impatiently counts off the time already passed since Troy's disappearance; he must wait only five years, nine months, and a few days. Gently, Gabriel points out that Bathsheba is still young and Boldwood may depend too much on promises, but Boldwood refuses to believe he could be so terribly disappointed as he was before. He is certain that if Bathsheba promises to marry him, she will keep her word.

(4)

Troy meets Pennyways at The White Hart tavern; Pennyways has not been able to see a lawyer about the legal aspects of Troy's return. Troy feels he is innocent of any law-breaking, but the ex-bailiff points out that his deception has made him a vagabond and that he could punished for desertion. Although Troy laughs at the possibility, he is still a bit worried; he asks about the connection between Bathsheba and Boldwood, but Pennyways has not been able to find out much, except that Boldwood was giving a party and that Bathsheba will attend. Gossip about the two can only report that she has not seen Boldwood since the fair and seems quite cold towards him.

Troy describes her to Pennyways as a splendid woman and tells him that he is glad he will soon make himself known to her. He asks Pennyways how she looked when he went by the farm; Pennyways reports that she looked at him as if he didn't exist and continued her supervision of the making of cider. When Pennyways tells him that Oak now manages both farms, Troy says that Gabriel probably finds it hard to manage Bathsheba. Pennyways does not agree, since Bathsheba depends so much on Gabriel, who still remains independent himself. Troy tells him that if Pennyways will help him, he, in turn, would help Pennyways make his peace with Bathsheba. By this time, Troy is ready for his work that evening.

(5)

Bathsheba is still reluctant to leave for the party and wishes that she did not look so well. Liddy tells her she looks as attractive as she did over a year ago when she so strongly defended Troy; she points out that Bathsheba's nervousness about the party heightens her beauty. She asks what Bathsheba would do if Boldwood should ask her to elope, and Bathsheba reminds her that she cannot marry for years and tells her that, if she does finally, it will be for reasons other than might be guessed. With this reply, she leaves for the party.

(6)

Boldwood tells Gabriel that his share in the farm is too small for all the work he does; his plan is to retire from managing the farm and eventually allow Gabriel to take over the full management. His hopes for Bathsheba make the world seem brighter to him, and he wants to share his happiness with Gabriel. Gabriel warns him not to plan too far ahead, since he had been sadly disappointed before. Boldwood admits that Gabriel is right, but he realizes that Gabriel's devotion to Bathsheba is more than just that of an employee and he would like to show his friendship and respect to his unsuccessful rival. Gabriel assures him that he can endure the pain as he leaves the feverishly excited Boldwood. Gabriel worries about the emotions that have made Boldwood so totally unlike his former self.

Boldwood remains in his room in a mood now rather solemn; he takes out a small box and opens it to look at a woman's ring set with diamonds. He stares at the obviously new ring for some time, when the sound of arriving carriages causes him to close the box and put it carefully away in his pocket. He is disappointed to find that Bathsheba has not yet arrived; although his reserved expression hides his feelings about her, he is obviously quite excited about something other than the party, as he greets his guests.

(7)

As he pulls on a heavy overcoat with a cape and huge collar which reaches to a cap pulled down over his ears, Troy asks Pennyways if he can be recognized. Pennyways approves the "disguise" and asks Troy why he will not write Bathsheba; in fact, he feels Troy is better off without a wife to worry about. Troy replies angrily that he is missing out on Bathsheba's obvious prosperity; since he saw her at the fair he had decided to return to her and would have by now had not Pennyways cautioned him about legal problems. It is too late to draw back now, since he has been seen about the village and recognized. He is angry at himself for running away, but he enjoys the thought of the dramatic impact his entry at the party will have, but then a sudden premonition of death strikes him.

Pennyways realizes that Troy's reconciliation with Bathsheba will mean a change of fortune for him, for better or for worse, so he begins to soften his comments about Bathsheba and agrees to do what Troy asks of him. Troy takes his leave and plans to arrive at Boldwood's party shortly before nine o'clock.

Comment

Hardy makes use of an interesting technique in this chapter, that of joining together seven small chapters to form the one larger one. This method offers the reader the opportunity to see developments progressing at three locations with Boldwood, Troy, and Bathsheba. In addition, Hardy can maintain suspense by moving from one character to another. The chapter ends precisely at the most exciting moment; the reader has been keyed to an excited pitch by the preparations for the party made by the three separate characters, and Hardy makes us eager to read on to discover the outcome of these preparations.

CHAPTER LIII: CONCURRITUR - HORAE MOMENTO

As the guests enter Boldwood's home, the light from the opening and closing of the door shines on a group of men discussing Troy's return. The gossipers agree that Bathsheba knows nothing about his reappearance and wonder if Troy means to avoid her or to do her some harm. One man seems to sympathize with Bathsheba, while another thinks her a fool for becoming involved with a man like Troy. As Jacob Smallbury approaches, the speakers are revealed as some of Boldwood's workers. Laban Tall joins them and asks them to keep quiet about Troy's return, since the report will hurt Bathsheba, if it is true or not. He insists that she has always been fair to him, despite the comments of men like Henery.

As the workers stand silently considering their own thoughts, Boldwood opens the door and comes down the path. They remain quiet as one of them points out that Boldwood might feel insulted that they had not come into the party sooner. They are unwilling eavesdroppers as Boldwood cries out his hopes for Bathsheba and of his torment at her keeping him in suspense. The men regret having overheard these private feelings and pity Boldwood, especially now that Troy has returned. Troy seems to have brought more trouble with him; the joy of the evening seems lost for the workers and they agree to go to Warren's malthouse before returning to Boldwood's.

As they approach, they discover Troy peering in the window, obviously intent on the conversation between Oak and the malster. The old man, gossiping about Boldwood's party, sees it as all being in Bathsheba's honor and comments that Boldwood is a fool to act this way for a woman who does not care for him. The men hurry back to the party; Tall is chosen to tell Bathsheba the news about Troy, but he cannot bring himself to spoil the party.

Bathsheba is still young enough to enjoy the party, but the conditions under which it is given tend to ruin it for her. She had decided to stay for only an hour and begins to take her leave when the time is up. Boldwood begs her to give him her promise to marry him at the end of the legal waiting period. When he agrees not to bring any pressure upon her during this time, she makes the long-awaited promise. He asks her to accept his ring, but she refuses, since she wants to keep the engagement a secret. He insists that she wear it only for the evening; she bends before his stronger will. Bathsheba stops near the bottom of the stairs to take a last look at the festivities before she leaves, but the guests seem to have broken up into small groups to discuss the news. Boldwood gaily inquires what has happened; the men are reluctant to tell him. Just as Laban is sent to tell Bathsheba, a stranger asking for Mrs. Troy is announced. Boldwood sends word for the stranger to join the party; as Troy enters, he is recognized by those who know of his return. Bathsheba is shocked; she can only stand and stare at the newcomer. Since he still does not recognize him, Boldwood cheerfully welcomes him; but then Troy is identified by his harsh laugh.

Troy turns to Bathsheba and orders her to come home with him. She is either too terrified or too surprised to move; a voice, hardly recognizable as Boldwood's, tells her to go with her husband. When Troy reaches out to pull her to him, she shrinks back. Her scream at his touch is followed by the sound of a gunshot;

Boldwood, looking like a madman, had fired at Troy and killed him. His attempt to kill himself is stopped by his workers. Boldwood crosses to Bathsheba, kisses her hand and then walks out into the darkness, before anyone can even think of stopping him.

Comment

This chapter might also serve as the **climax** of the book, since the action from this point on is "falling action," and the height of excitement and pitch of intensity is reached at this point. Boldwood is the director of the events Troy's return sets in motion; having carried out his part in Bathsheba's story, he removes himself from the action.

Hardy has set the scene for the acceptance of Boldwood's role as murderer very carefully. He throws out several hints of Boldwood's growing lack of mental stability; he often repeats that Boldwood is a much changed man; indeed, Bathsheba fears he will lose his mind if she doesn't accept him, and Troy had inquired of Coggan about a history of insanity in Boldwood's family. This development towards Troy's murder is a perfect example of Hardy's craftsmanship in putting the plot together; details which seem unimportant at the time are suddenly seen as threads which lead to a later important event. There is very little in the way of action that is wasted in this novel.

CHAPTER LIV: AFTER THE SHOCK

Deliberately, and with firm, even steps, Boldwood walks to Casterbridge and surrenders himself at the jail. The news of disaster spreads quickly; Gabriel arrives a few minutes after Boldwood's departure to find the guests bewildered and terrified. Bathsheba calmly holds Troy's body in her arms; she sends Gabriel for the doctor even though it is too late. Impelled by the quiet power of her words, Gabriel hurries off on her errand. When he returns with the doctor, he is told that Bathsheba has taken Troy back to her farm; the doctor is angry since there will probably have on to be an investigation, and he did not want the body moved. They continue to Weatherbury Farm; Liddy tells them that Bathsheba is upstairs with the body. They find Troy's body carefully prepared for burial. The doctor expresses his admiration for her iron-like strength of spirit, but Bathsheba faints-no longer able to endure the strain. The doctor's attention is diverted to Bathsheba. Liddy nurses her all night long, as she continues to insist that everything is her fault.

Comment

This chapter is a quiet release from the tension and excitement of the previous one. The action slows down and the characters themselves act quietly. Even the dialogue seems spoken in a whisper, like the muted tones at a funeral. This pause serves to allow the reader to "catch his breath" after the **climax** before proceeding with the rest of the story.

CHAPTER LV: THE MARCH FOLLOWING - "BATHSHEBA BOLDWOOD"

In March of the next year a group of men are waiting on Yalbury Hill for the arrival of one of the two judges of the western circuit. The judge changes carriages at this point and rides on toward Casterbridge followed by most of the group, except for the men from Weatherbury Farm. The men discuss the trial that is about to start; they agree to stay at home and not upset Boldwood by their presence. The next day they wait anxiously for the news.

Meanwhile, a discovery was made that afternoon which helped to explain Boldwood's mental state, and this gave the rustics something to help keep their minds off the trial. Since the day at the fair, Boldwood's mental collapse was suspected, especially by Gabriel and Bathsheba. The proof that his mind was crazed by love and fear of losing that love was found in a locked closet. Boldwood had spent the time from September to Christmas buying dresses, furs and jewelry, which were carefully packed away, with a date six years from the present marked and labeled "Bathsheba Boldwood."

Oak returns from the trial to report that Boldwood had pleaded guilty and has been sentenced to die. The conviction that Boldwood is mentally unstable grows; once given the suggestion of insanity, many instances of his mental deterioration are recalled. Accordingly, a petition addressed to the Home Secretary listing all of this evidence is prepared and signed by those interested in Boldwood's fate.

In Weatherbury, the outcome of the petition was eagerly awaited; up until the Friday afternoon before the execution was set, no word came. Gabriel visits the jail to bid good-by to Boldwood and sees the carpenters preparing the platform for the execution. Gabriel returns without any hopeful news. He asks Laban Tall to ride to Casterbridge and stay until at least eleven o'clock, for if the reprieve is not received by then, there is no chance of its coming at all. Liddy hopes that Bathsheba will be spared the anguish of Boldwood's execution; she is a bit better physically than she was at Christmastime, but Boldwood's death would be too much for her to bear.

Laban leaves for Casterbridge and, at eleven o'clock, most of Bathsheba's workers wait on the road for his return. Gabriel's conscience tells him that Boldwood should die, but he pities the poor man who was once so worthy of respect. To their relief, Laban finally arrives, and reports that Boldwood has been spared; he will remain in prison "during Her Majesty's pleasure." Coggan voices joy and their feeling that good has triumphed over evil.

Comment

A severe retribution for Troy's murder would seem out of place and even unjust. Boldwood's stay of execution is not the **deus ex machina** technique again, since the evidence for Boldwood's madness has been carefully developed within the plot. Boldwood's punishment would not "fit the crime" if he had been executed.

CHAPTER LVI: BEAUTY IN LONELINESS - AFTER ALL

By spring, Bathsheba was better, but she remained in the house for the most part and saw no one; even Liddy could not comfort her. As the summer drew near, she went out more and began to take an interest in the farm. One evening in August she came into the village for the first time since Christmas. As she entered the graveyard and walked toward Fanny's grave, she heard the church choir practicing. Under the inscription ordered by Troy, another has been added: "In the same Grave Lie the Remains of the Aforesaid Francis Troy who died December 24th, 18____, Aged 26 years."

As she reads these words, the organist starts to play another hymn; Bathsheba walks to the front of the church and listens to the words of "Lead, Kindly Light." She is strangely moved by the hymn and begins to cry; the words seem to be deeply meaningful to her. She does not notice the approach of Gabriel who tells her he has come for the practice, and then she starts to leave. He lingers to talk to her and she tells him that she has come to see the tombstone, and that it seems years since the unhappy events of last Christmas.

The two begin to walk home and Gabriel informs her that he is thinking of leaving England for California the next spring; she asks what she will do without him, since she has been dependent on him for so long. He seems insistent on leaving however, despite her pleas.

Bathsheba considers this new disaster and with great pain she comes to believe she has lost Gabriel's love. During the next three weeks, she notices more signs of his apparent loss of interest. He hardly ever comes to the farm, and sends messages or notes when he needs her instructions. Through fall and on toward Christmas, her sadness at Gabriel's loss seems to outweigh her memories of the last sad Christmas. The day after Christmas, Gabriel sends a note informing her he will not renew his engagement to work for her on the next Lady's Day (March 25).

Bathsheba breaks down and cries over the letter; she had always considered Gabriel as the mainstay of her life. She becomes so desolate in thinking she has lost her truest friend, that she walks into Gabriel's house shortly after sunset. She is nervous about this meeting and not quite sure it is proper to call on a bachelor in his home, even if he is her manager. Gabriel, in turn, is awkward at greeting her. Bathsheba tells him of her grief at his leaving and asks if she has offended him. He explains that he is not leaving England and that he will take over Little

Weatherbury Farm on May 1st. He would have stayed on as her manager, but gossip about them might ruin her reputation; Gabriel is reported as waiting for Boldwood's farm with the hope of eventually winning Bathsheba. She is surprised and calls the notion absurd and too soon to think of. He seizes her words "too absurd" and agrees that she is the last person he would think of marrying. This remark upsets her; she tearfully insists she only meant that it was too soon for her to marry. He replies tenderly that things could be different if he only knew that she would marry him someday. She says he'll never know, because he will not ask; she reminds him that she was his first sweetheart. Gabriel regrets her thinking he has stopped loving her, for he had only wanted to spare her the gossip about them.

As she starts to leave, she tells him how glad she is that she came and that the misunderstanding between them has been cleared up; she adds that it seems as if she had come to court him. Oak remarks that this is as it should be; he had promised never again to ask her to marry him. He had patiently waited all this time, and she should not begrudge him one visit. He walks back to her house with her; instead of exchanging pretty phrases, they talk of the farm he will soon manage. They have no need of exaggerated protests of love; their love has developed through similarity of interests and through sharing confidences and troubles. It has transcended mere infatuation or passion.

Comment

The developments of this chapter again suit the happy mood of the book as a whole. Gabriel's patience must be justly rewarded. The reader remembers that Gabriel has sworn that he would not offer marriage to Bathsheba again; his words to Bathsheba reminding her of his long devotion are not a rebuke, but a statement that things are finally what they should be. The remark indicates that Bathsheba is no longer the vain young lady of the earlier proposal; the new Bathsheba is not too proud to accept Gabriel-she even suggests the marriage.

The lasting strength of this marriage is suggested by their lack of need for "pretty phrases." The situation is totally opposite that of Bathsheba's former marriage, which relied so heavily on flattery and passion.

CHAPTER LVII: A FOGGY NIGHT AND MORNING - CONCLUSION

Sometime after Bathsheba's visit to Gabriel, the two plan a private wedding. A few days later, Gabriel meets Coggan and walks with him to the village; he explains he is going to see Laban (recently appointed clerk of the parish). Gabriel finally confides that Bathsheba and he will be married the next morning and requests him to keep the news secret.

Coggan is surprised only at the secrecy, for he thought of the match for some time. Coggan reminds him that Tall's wife will spread the news throughout the parish, and offers to ask Laban to see Gabriel outside. Susan tells him that Laban is out, however; Coggan is finally instructed to tell her to ask Laban to meet Bathsheba at the church the next day. Coggan adds that the matter involves Bathsheba's contract with another farmer to take shares for a long period of time. Their visit to the vicar is less troublesome and arouses no curiosity.

Bathsheba sleeps little that night, and rises long before the hour at which she was to be called; she tells Liddy only that Oak is coming for dinner. When Liddy worries about her reputation, she whispers the truth to her. The morning is damp and dismal but Gabriel and Bathsheba set out cheerfully, arm-in-arm for the first time in their lives. Bathsheba is plainly dressed, but her happiness restores color to her face; Gabriel's request that she wear her hair as she did when he first saw her suggests that she is not old at twenty-four, nor an entirely different girl from the one he watched on Norcombe Hill.

Only Liddy, Laban and the parson are at the church; the two are married quietly and Gabriel moves into Bathsheba's house, which is a more practical arrangement. As Bathsheba pours him some tea, they hear the noise of a cannon firing and trumpets blowing. The villagers have come to celebrate the wedding; the noise is identified as the music from the Weatherbury band. Gabriel invites Mark Clark, Jan Coggan and the others in for some refreshments; they however promise to call on the two sometime soon and ask that refreshments be sent instead to Warren's malthouse. Gabriel's casual use of "my wife" when referring to Bathsheba impresses the merry villagers; Gabriel sounds like a husband of long standing, rather than a newlywed. Gabriel and Bathsheba are quite amused by this joking as their friends take their leave.

Comment

The story could end in no other way than by the happy prospect of a long, serene life for Bathsheba and Gabriel. Each has weathered many trials and learned much from them; they are justly entitled to their happiness. Bathsheba had never expected to find happiness in marriage, but she finally marries for love, and not infatuation or guilt. The novel begins and ends with Gabriel, who moves from modest success, through failure, and then returns to happiness and prosperity. He would warmly agree that refreshments had never been sent to Warren's for a happier occasion.

It is fitting that the novel ends with a comment from the most endearing of the rustics, Poorgrass, since the novel is a pastoral one and the rustics have had their share in the development of the plot, and especially Joseph, whose lapses into "seeing double" provided for the circumstances by which Bathsheba matures and finds happiness.

FAR FROM THE MADDING CROWD

CHARACTER ANALYSES

GABRIEL OAK

Gabriel's appearance marks him as a man who is not concerned with modern developments or surface attraction. His clothes are as humble and traditional as his interests.

His trust does not lie in the machine, or man-made world, but in nature; his closeness to nature is symbolized by his name.

His devotion to Bathsheba is marked by a patient acceptance, both of her faults and her need to mature. His sense of responsibility and skill in farming causes her to trust him implicitly; for all of his gifts, Gabriel is not proud. He realizes that fortune is apt to change quickly (as it does in his own life) and he does not resent Boldwood's assuming his place at the sheepshearing feast. He accepts trouble or good fortune as it comes, without question, and he can even be cheerful in difficult times, as when he plays the flute at the hiring fair despite his disappointment at not finding a place.

All of Gabriel's good qualities can be summarized in his serene acceptance of his limitations, as well as of his talents. He knows how far his skills can take him, and does not make himself unhappy by reaching for that which is beyond his grasp. He respects himself as a man and as an individual, and this dignity causes the rustics to admire and respect him. They do not begrudge him his advancement, but feel he has earned it himself and that his prosperity is a just reward.

His conscience is moral and upright; he knows that Boldwood should be punished for murdering Troy, yet his compassion causes him to hope for Boldwood's reprieve. He cannot bring himself to lie to Bathsheba or to flatter her; he answers her requests for his opinion simply, honestly and frankly, no matter what it costs him in her good favor. This sense of the "rightness" of things makes him refuse her first request to save the injured sheep, and to allow her to make the first gesture toward their eventual marriage.

BATHSHEBA

Bathsheba's beauty and charming ways endear her to most people, even Gabriel who is not blind to her faults. She is thoroughly independent in spirit and insists on having her own way, an admirable quality that unfortunately lapses into pride and vanity at the beginning of the story. But it must be remembered that Bathsheba is still a young girl at this point and maturity and trial will lessen her faults and create an admirable woman of character and dignity.

At first, she is inclined to be impetuous; she acts without reflection (she sends the foolish valentine to Boldwood, for example). She likes to be admired and flattered and so becomes a perfect prey for Troy, who dazzles her by his sweet words and glittering swordplay.

Just like a child, she can display flashes of temper and bewilder poor Liddy with her outbursts. She balances this, however, by her genuine regret for her lack of control. She is intensely female in her defense of Troy, as Liddy points out, and in her sudden desire to be admired and respected by her neighboring farmers (which causes her to set out to win Boldwood's attention). Her sudden rise to prosperity in inheriting her uncle's farm gives her wonderful chance to display her childish wish to command and to require respect; the sense of power which this position of authority brings, she eventually learns, must be tempered with kindness and understanding.

As she matures, she becomes genuinely concerned with other people and learns to respect important things, such as her friendship with Gabriel. Her charity toward Fanny is exemplary; despite her disappointment at Troy's bond with Fanny, she does her best to treat Fanny's corpse with consideration and kindness.

The best evaluation of her is Hardy's: "She was of the stuff of which great men's mothers are made."

BOLDWOOD

Boldwood appears on the surface to be reserved, staid and remote, but submerged within him is a disastrous whirlpool of emotion that finally erupts with the provocation of Bathsheba.

Respected as a "gentleman" by the community, he is like Edward Arlington Robinson's Richard Cory who "fluttered pulses" when he greeted his neighbors, but who rarely mixed in their company. The villagers are astonished when Boldwood plans a party, but the reader is aware that Boldwood's remoteness is ending when he joins Bathsheba's song at the shearing feast.

His love for Bathsheba is expressed by an overwhelming desire to possess her; he becomes so preoccupied with this one desire that his rational mind deserts him. He allows his farm to run down; he "lowers" himself in his own eyes by confiding his troubles to an outsider, Gabriel. He becomes reckless when Bathsheba seems so close to his grasp; his wild joy and fear at losing her again causes his workers to pity him.

His obsession allows him the secret delight of buying gifts for Bathsheba, including an expensive ring, but it blinds him to the fact that his selfish determination and demands for justice are forcing Bathsheba into a marriage she detests. She is overwhelmed by the force of his passion and by the feelings of guilt he raises. Had the marriage ever taken place, Bathsheba would probably have been destroyed in her misery, and Boldwood disenchanted by his prize.

It is his genuine kindness, especially early in the novel (in his treatment of and concern for Fanny), however, as well as his past responsibility as a farmer that serves to maintain some respect and compassion from his associates. It is rather sad that few real friends can be found to sign the petition for his reprieve, rather, it is only those truly interested in his fate who work to save him. The villagers who tactfully stay away from his trial and anxiously await news of his trial are remembering the old Boldwood and not the madman; they are genuinely concerned for the man who has so "changed" from what he once was.

TROY

He would seem one-sided in his villainy, had he not felt some genuine remorse at Fanny's death and repented his harsh treatment of her. If Bathsheba matures beyond her impulsiveness of her early actions, Troy never does. He decides to claim Bathsheba by a theatrical entrance at Boldwood's party, and never considers her feelings as he kisses Fanny and her child, and then departs without further word.

Unlike Gabriel, he is never satisfied, but is continually restless and unable to feel peace and security (from his first morning as master of Weatherbury Farm he plans to change and "modernize"). Like his skill at the sword exercise, he is attractive and thrilling, but rather shallow and empty. Furthermore, he feels free to lie to women, and he is almost contemptible in refusing to end Bathsheba's anguish at his loss, until he is sure he will not be burdened with her support.

Like Bathsheba, he insists on independence and freedom; unlike her, he never realizes the responsibilities this independence involves. He enjoys his authority as master of the farm, but it is only a role for him and he is not concerned with the well-being of his workers, or with the prosperity of the farm.

To be sure, he is to be admired for his stand on refusing Boldwood's "bargain," but had he not married Bathsheba (and been assured of financial security), he might have been tempted to take Boldwood's money as a "bonus" for marrying Fanny, as he had originally intended.

FAR FROM THE MADDING CROWD

CRITICAL COMMENTARY

GENERAL ESTIMATE

Far From the Madding Crowd can hardly be regarded as Hardy's greatest work. At its best, it is a pleasant, restful book, which offers the peaceful repose of an idyllic view of rustic England. Critics who look for more than a quiet pastoral setting and a well-constructed plot are apt to be disappointed. Henry James, for example, missed the strong points of the novel in his condemnation of Hardy. Lascelle Abercrombie, on the other hand, understood Hardy's choice of the pastoral, and appreciated both the description of nature and the comedy presented by "the band of laborers," which he terms Shakespearian, for its faithful rendering of the lives of the rustics.

Among more modern critics, the novel receives either scant attention in any general consideration of Hardy's work, or brings agreement on the virtues (such as the picture of rustic life) and vices (preoccupation with plot). These modern critics generally agree on terming Hardy a "good transitional novelist."

His long life span caused Hardy to straddle both the Victorian and the modern periods; both are represented in his work. He is traditional novelist in his carefully constructed plots, as Albert Guerard points out, and yet modern in his interest in the psychological development of his character, and most important for the work of later novelists, in his use of the novel as a reflection of modern problems. Guerard adds that Hardy pioneered in developing symbolic and allegoric levels in the novel form; he agrees with Morton Zabel that Hardy's work prepared the way for the works of Joyce, Proust, Gide and Kafka.

It is surprising that Hardy can also join the modern novelists through his love and respect for the past greatness of rustic England. With Lawrence, Ford Madox Ford and E. M. Forster, he contrasts this serene world, so fond of tradition and permanence, with the busy, crass commercial world that was slowly destroying the old world. Wing develops this by pointing out that Pennyways, in *Far From the Madding Crowd*, represents a kind of canker eating into this healthy way of life, and thus he can further be considered a symbol of the current destructive force.

Since we are sure of Hardy's acceptance as a great novelist, it would be well to consider here the features of his novels (and particularly *Far From the Madding Crowd*), that have been most often discussed by his critics.

PLOT

James Wright joins the other critics who consider Hardy's plots as symmetrical; Wright goes a step further and actually diagrams the plot of *Far From the Madding Crowd*. Joseph Warren Beach agrees that the plot is essential to the nature of Hardy's novels, and goes one step further in saying it becomes their raison d'etre. Beach does add that plot discrepancies do exist, and that Hardy is forced to use techniques such as the deus ex machina for this reason; the critic poses this question for consideration: Did the setting exist for the plot, or the plot for the setting? At least in the case of *Far From the Madding Crowd,* Beach thinks that the novel was planned with the setting in mind, and then the plot was suited to the setting. This might help to account for the need to use outside forces to solve his plot problems.

Both Abercrombie and E. M. Forster praise Hardy's plot structure, however; Abercrombie speaks of the "lucid intricacy" and "richness of incident," while Forster points out that Hardy carefully arranges events with emphasis on causality. He would probably take exception to Beach's point about the importance of the setting in considering the major novel, since he sees the ground plan of the novel as the plot, with the characters ordered to acquiesce to its demands; but he does not consider *Far From the Madding Crowd* separately from the major novels, as Beach does. A recent criticism of plot structure (by Walter O'Grady) sets Hardy below James in integrating plot with the novel, since his events flow "outward" and "backward" (or, in other words, the causality of action depends on previous action-which Abercrombie does not see as a fault).

From out of this apparent confusion of ideas on plot, what common ground can we find? We can safely affirm, that for better or worse, Hardy's plots are symmetrically arranged; there is an obvious pattern to be noticed in the novels, and that each action proceeds from a former action, and depends upon it. If we join the more modern critics, whose interests are in features other than plot, we must look further for Hardy's stature as novelist.

POETRY

In Aspects of the Novel, E. M. Forster gives us an important clue in evaluating Hardy: he is essentially a poet. Guerard joins Forster in suggesting the importance of this connection between novelist and poet. It is in this use of poetry in the novel that Hardy joins the modern novelists, for poetry in this analysis, is extended to Hardy's use of language and symbol in his novels.

Wright agrees that the use of poetic language adds another dimension to Hardy's work; the novelist and poet were not at war in the same man, but Hardy makes use of his poetic language in his novels. He adds that the nature-descriptions are not mere padding, but are embodied in the spirit of *Far From the Madding Crowd*.

Hardy's poetic language includes his use of local dialect (which Abercrombie feels is effective, if not accurate), and his use of allusive language to add a subtle strength to his novels. *Far From the Madding Crowd* is rich in **allusion**, both to Biblical and to literary sources. Beach finds the Biblical **allusions** far more effective in his novel, since it seems to fit more naturally into the simple life of the rustics. The literary **allusions** seem more forced, and sometimes involve a ridiculous comparison (Gabriel's watching of Bathsheba is compared to Satan's first gaze at Paradise in Milton's *Paradise Lost*). A particularly amusing Biblical **allusion** is made when Liddy refers to the approaching rustics as "Philistines."

Most recently, those critics interested in Hardy's poetic techniques employed in his novels, have been considering the symbolic level in his works. "Oak" for the choice of Gabriel's name is obvious; but there are more subtle uses, such as the "mirror" and the "sword" that Richard C. Carpenter discusses.

CHARACTERIZATION

If the psychological depths involved in Hardy's later novels are not to be found in *Far From the Madding Crowd,* we can at least find consolation in his effective blending of his rustic characters with the setting and plot. Guerard's statement about the compact personality of the rustics supports Abercrombie's perception of the "action in a group" by the rustics. In this novel, perhaps more than several of the later novels, the rustics act as chorus (or general comment) on the action; in cases such as Poorgrass's neglect of Fanny's body, the rustics actually become involved in the action and direct its progress.

In viewing the rustics, Guerard tells us that they have only a past history, and little present involvement; they are immune to suffering and change, and their stability weighs the action and characterization. George Wing agrees by stating that the rustics are a personification of old ways and superstitions. All of the critics agree that the rustics add strength and depth to this novel.

Wright goes further in praising Oak, and especially his stability and patient endurance, than many other critics have. It is through Gabriel's "wise passiveness" that the other characters and events are measured. Even Troy's rather one-sided villainy is rejected by Wing; Troy is aggressively masculine, and his faithlessness and callousness can be viewed as a rejection of female domination. A hint of even psychological probing can be found in the portrait of Boldwood. Thus, it is fairly obvious that Hardy's characterization deserves some approval and it does assist us in assessing Hardy's strength as a novelist.

HUMOR

It may seem strange to consider humor as a feature in Hardy's novels, especially since he is often termed a "Victorian pessimist." In his later novels, Hardy often manages to lash out at the dominating outside forces which control the action; a hint of this can be seen in the mischance that sends Fanny to the wrong church. If not as apparent in the other novels, humor is a vital factor in assessing the worth of *Far From the Madding Crowd*.

The humor suggested by the rustics' conversations and actions is obvious. When Cainy Bell returns from Bath to tell of his discovery of Bathsheba and Troy, the reader's curiosity is strained to the utmost. Gabriel and his fellow workers wait patiently for the news as Cainy alternately chokes and sputters. Then the rustics join the fun and question Cainy about Bath, much to Gabriel's consternation. Wing points out this **episode** as one of the most humorous in the book, but we have many; Coggan and Poorgrass at the fair, Laban Tall's troubles with his domineering wife, and the merry-making at the shearing feast, among others. Abercrombie calls the rich vein of humor in this novel "Shakespearian," and adds that the humor suits the rustics, since it is far from the sophisticated wit of urban life. Grimsditch joins the general chorus of praise by calling the humor "rare whimsical comedy."

IRONY

Irony is also involved in the novel; grim humor pervades the reaction to Troy's disastrous planting of flowers on Fanny's grave. Beach is credited with pointing out the **irony** in the title itself; even in this peaceful setting, "ignoble strife" appears and complicates life.

SUMMARY

However sharply the critics disagree on the value of Hardy's symmetrically arranged plots, general agreement can be found on these positive features; Hardy's use of the rustics is effective, his poetic language (especially **allusion** and symbolism) has added another dimension to his novels, and his humor lightens the sad events of the stories. Most of these features, along with an abiding interest in England's traditions, have helped to make Hardy a major novelist.

Far From the Madding Crowd remains a minor novel; perhaps it lacks the stature and depth of the later novels, precisely because Hardy was developing his techniques in this early work. Wright, however, feels that there is a quality about the novel that endears it to most of its readers. Perhaps it is liked because of its language, or its humor; Wright seems to enjoy it for its characterization, especially that of Gabriel, "the genius of the places that are fresh and green." Whatever the quality, or combination of qualities, the novel is still being read and enjoyed; and, as Wright says, "There is something about the book that inspires people to love it, and love ... does not yield to ... even judicious argument."

FAR FROM THE MADDING CROWD

ESSAY QUESTIONS AND ANSWERS

Question: How does the pastoral setting affect the development of the novel.

Answer: As its name implies, the pastoral novel concerns itself with rustic life and the lives of simple people. It gives the author a chance to explore the charm of the native customs, shown in this novel, for example, by the warm, gay shearing feast. Terrible storms or fires might temporarily destroy the peaceful life, but troubles are balanced by cheerful evenings at Warren's, fondly recalling old times and old faces. Nature is at its best; cold winters are not destructive but present the opportunity of enjoying the observation of the constellations on a bright, cold night. Springs and summers bring days of fresh, green beauty.

Because of this connection with this "primitive," peaceful world, the pastoral loses its contact with the "real" world. By its identification as "pastoral," the reader must accept the **conventions** offered; he enters another world and cannot judge the novel in terms of hard **realism**. We find the characters generally good-natured, willing workers, content with their lot (Henery Fray is an exception, but then he is not malicious and his faults are amusing). They sometimes seem "too good to be true," especially Gabriel, whose nobility of character allies him more to the hero of melodrama than "real life." But we have been warned by the pastoral setting not to expect realism in characterization and do not look for it in plot, either. Sailors "just happen" to save Troy from drowning; Boldwood is saved by a last-minute reprieve, and the patient Gabriel wins Bathsheba.

Hardy has purposely chosen the pastoral setting, partly from his nostalgia for the way of life that was rapidly disappearing, even as he wrote about it, and partly out of respect for the tradition-bound villagers. Time has little meaning for the people of Weatherbury Farm; fifty or one hundred years see little changed. Troy seems doubly villainous when he plans to "modernize," the reader is confirmed in assuming that the sheep shearing, which has been conducted in the same way for centuries will continue as long as these rustics survive. England seems at the height of its health, strength and power, when it is peopled by characters such as Gabriel. Hardy's capturing of this serenity and idyllic happiness serves both as a contrast to the present commercialized spirit and as a warning of the hazards to be faced, if this life is ignored or lost.

Question: Describe the importance of **irony** in the novel.

Answer: **Irony**, in its context of "grim humor," enhances the enjoyment of the novel. Prophetic warnings and curses are uttered and carried out, in a way not often contemplated by their speaker.

The sense of tragedy is deepened by a sad twist to a situation, such as Fanny's going to the wrong church for her wedding. A more patient man than Troy would have appreciated the absurdity of blaming Fanny; she seems constantly maneuvered by an outside force. The few minutes' delay costs her Troy and even her life; Troy's whole life is changed by his angry dismissal of her.

Troy fails to appreciate this outside force, until it turns on him and ruins his carefully planted flowers. At the same time, the reader observes the tragedy of this destruction and the grim joke on Troy for his belated kindness to Fanny.

This grim humor is gentler when dealing with Bathsheba's embarrassment at having to send for Gabriel, the only one who can save her sheep, just after she has dismissed him. Both she and Gabriel do not try to fight this outside force, but accept it stoically.

It is also ironic that Bathsheba should send her valentine to the one man who could not treat it lightly, and that she should have to pay so heavily for her childish whim. It is a reversal, however, in that this guilt and repentance help her to become a better person. By the end of the novel, the girl who stared at herself in the mirror with such satisfaction becomes the woman who wishes she did not look so attractive as she prepares for Boldwood's party.

Irony lends a sad humor to the events of the novel and deepens the sense of tragedy and loss, as the characters involve themselves in events they cannot really foresee.

Question: What role does nature play in the story?

Answer: Hardy fully utilizes his poetic talents in descriptions of nature. His language becomes poetic as he describes the beautiful dawn and spring days. Furthermore, the descriptions are integral in creating the atmosphere of the events occurring in the shadow of nature; the reader grasps the "feel" of the gloomy weather, as Poorgrass brings Fanny's body home, or as the strong rain washes away the flowers from her grave. The descriptions assume an almost symbolic level, as in the sound of the water outside Troy's barracks.

The force of nature can be damaging to those who do not relate to it. Gabriel is rewarded for his contact with the world of nature with an ability to observe and control it, which wins him the admiration and approval of Bathsheba and her workers. Troy and Boldwood are impervious to nature's charms; they battle it, and are destroyed by it. Boldwood neglects his farm, Troy nearly causes catastrophe by not covering the ricks, and rain washes away his only attempt at relating to nature. Troy is nearly drowned at sea and is destroyed by an "unnatural" force in Boldwood.

For those who live in harmony with nature, as Hardy pleads, there is a serene, happy life, as Bathsheba eventually learns. She trusts Gabriel's judgment in the natural world and finds happiness, she is alert to the beauty of the dawn after her tragic discovery, and is refreshed by it. It will be remembered that she ignores the night's beginning to settle about her as she considers searching for Troy at Bath (and is eventually made unhappy by that meeting), and that she is bored when caring for her aunt's cows. Anyone who could so enjoy a morning ride, however, as Bathsheba's joyous trip to the mill, is not totally devoid of feeling for nature.

Question: What effect did the serialization in the *Cornhill Magazine* have on the development of the plot?

Answer: In the interest of good serialization. Hardy had to shape the novel into **episodes** and use methods of keeping up reader interest. He does this by techniques such as hiding the identity of the character involved in the action with a known character. Several times Fanny appears as "a woman" who meets Troy; Hardy does not identify the soldier waiting to be married until the end of the chapter. Gabriel helps an unknown farmer, who turns out to be Bathsheba; he and Coggan pursue a "robber" on the road to Bath, only to find Bathsheba driving her own gig. Hardy also employed the device of a climax at the end of each **episode** to insure the reader's purchase of the next installment.

He obviously had to have an outline of the development of the story as a whole, in order to arrange his **episodes** toward a logical conclusion. This careful structure of the plot makes the book "symmetrical" in action (much admired by Hardy's contemporaries, even if modern audiences seem not very interested in it). The novel is also necessarily "episodic," that is, capable of being broken up into recognizable blocks of action. Hardy was also free to arrange a change in locality or character involvement as he opened each new episode.

Perhaps it was the magazine serialization, as much as the pastoral setting, that caused Hardy to arrange outcomes as he did; reader interest would demand "poetic justice," in that Boldwood and Troy must suffer, as Gabriel and Bathsheba prosper. This involves **deus ex machina** complications, which are not always beneficial to the novel.

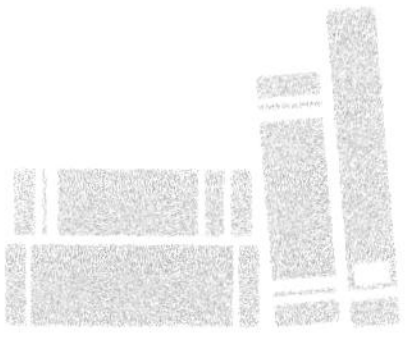

GLOSSARY

Acheron: River of woe in Hades.

Aldebaran: Red star in the eye of Taurus; brightest star in Hyades.

All-Fours: card game.

Aphrodite: Greek goddess of love and beauty; Roman Counterpart: Venus.

Ararat: Genesis: Noah's ark comes to rest on this mountain.

Arcadian: any scene of simple, pleasant, quiet life, usually pastoral.

Ashtoreth: (Hebrew) goddess Astarte, Phoenician goddess of love, fertility.

Bailiff: custodian, overseer, manager of an estate.

Balboa, Vasco de (1475–1517): Spanish explorer, discoverer of the Pacific Ocean.

Bath: city in southwestern England, famous watering spot.

Bear: Northern Constellation.

Beaumont And Fletcher: early seventeenth-century dramatists.

Betelgeux: variable red giant star of first magnitude. near Orion.

Biffins: red cooking apples.

Blasted: withered, blighted, injured by air.

Candlemas: February 2nd, Feast of the Purification of the Blessed Virgin Mary.

Capella: a star of first magnitude, near Auriga.

Cassiopeia: northern constellation.

Castor And Pollux: two bright stars in Gemini.

Chamfer: fluted surface formed by cutting away angle formed by two faces of a piece of timber or stone.

Charles's Wain: the Big Dipper.

Costard: English variety of large apple.

Cretan: (from the expression "lie like a Cretan") Cretans had a reputation for lying; an ancient sophism was based on this reputation.

Cyclops: race of giants with one eye in the middle of the forehead; they were shepherds, according to Homer.

Daniel: Hebrew prophet.

Diana: Roman virgin-huntress goddess.

Dog Star: Sirius.

Dou, Gerard: Dutch painter (1613–1675).

Drabbet: coarse, drab linen fabric used for smocks, etc.

Dryad: Greek nymphs whose lives were dependent on the trees they inhabited.

Elymas: sorcerer and false prophet.

Eros: Greek god of love; Roman counterpart, Cupid.

Espalier: railing or trellis on which fruit trees or shrubs are trained.

Eve of St. Thomas: either the feast of St. Thomas the Apostle (Dec. 21) or St. Thomas of Canterbury (Dec. 29). Since it was supposed to be the shortest day of the year, Hardy probably means the former feast.

Felon: inflammation of a finger or toe.

Flaxman, John: English sculptor (1755–1826).

Gig: light, two-wheeled one-horse carriage.

Gilpin's Rig: refers to a humorous poem by William Cowper, English poet (1731–1800).

Gonzalo: character in Shakespeare's *The Tempest*, Act I, scene 1; he prays for a dry death.

Guildenstern: character in Shakespeare's *Hamlet* (II, ii source of quotation).

Gurgoyle (gargoyle): waterspouts often grotesquely carved.

Hades: hell, lower regions (Greek).

Hippocrates: 460? - 377 B.C., Greek physician, Father of Medicine.

Hobbema, Meyndert: Dutch painter (1638–1709).

Horeb: also called Sinai; mountain where the Ten Commandments were given to Moses. Hustings: platforms from which candidates for Parliament were formerly nominated.

Hylas: a young armor-bearer, a favorite of Hercules captured by the Naiads at Mysii.

Ixion: King of Thessalians, bound to an endlessly revolving wheel.

Jacob: Genesis: Jacob worked for Laban 7 years to win Rachel.

Jove: Roman God Jupiter: Greek counterpart, Zeus.

Juggernaut: massive force that advances, irresistibly crushing whatever is in its path.

Lady Day: Annunciation Day - March 25.

Laodicean: lukewarm, or indifferent, as were the Christians of ancient Laodicea.

Lettre De Cachet: sealed letter.

Lucina: Greek goddess of childbirth, identified with Juno.

Majolica: variety of Renaissance Italian pottery, glazed and richly colored and ornamented.

Melpomene: muse of tragedy.

Mercury: Roman god-messenger.

Metheglin: beverage made of fermented honey and water, mead.

Minerva: Roman goddess, Greek counterpart, Athena; goddess of wisdom in peace and skill at war.

Moses: Hebrew prophet and lawgiver, led Israelites out of Egypt.

Napoleon At St. Helena: island in the Atlantic where the French general and ruler died May 5, 1821.

Nebula: one of large class of celestial structures.

Nicene Creed: profession of belief formulated and decreed by the Council of Nicaea in 325 A.D.

Night Thoughts: gloomy poem by Edward Young (1683–1765).

Nijni Novgorod: site of famous fair; the city was an important trade center especially in the thirteenth and fourteenth centuries; it is located in North Russia.

North Star: polestar, star toward which the axis of the earth points.

Nymphean: lesser goddesses, represented as beautiful maidens who lived in mountains, forests and waters.

Ochreous: yellowish color.

Olympus: mountain in Macedonia, mythical home of the Greek gods.

Orion: constellation on the equator, represented by a hunter with belt and sword.

Palimpsest: parchment, tablet, etc., which has been used two or three times, the earlier writing having been erased.

Pattens: type of overshoe with high wooden sole, raises the feet from water or mud.

Philistines: used here by Liddy to describe the rustics as uncultured, unenlightened.

Pilgrim's Progress: allegoric work by John Bunyan (1628–1688).

Pillars of Hercules: two promontories (high point of land or rock) at the eastern end of the Strait of Gibraltar. It is fabled that Hercules set them there.

Plantation: grove, or group of planted trees.

Pleiades: group of stars in constellation Taurus.

Poussin, Nicolas: French painter (1594–1655).

Purification Day: February 2 (feast of the Blessed Virgin Mary).

Rick: stack or pile of grain, straw or hay in the open air.

Ruysdael, Jacob: Dutch painter (1628?–1682).

Saint-Simon, Comte Claude: French philosopher and socialist (1760–1825).

Sengreen: houseleek.

Sexagesima: second Sunday before Lent.

Shadrach, Meshach, Abednego: Daniel: Nebuchadnezzar sent these three young men to die in a fiery furnace, but they were saved.

Shimei, Son Of Gera: man who opposed David and cursed him.

Sirius: star of constellation Canis Major, brightest star in heavens.

Spectator: periodical by Addison and Steele, issued March, 1711 to Dec. 1712.

Square Of Pegasus: one of the northern constellations, presented as a winged horse.

Staddles: lower parts of stack, or its supporting frame or base.

"Swoln With Wind And The Rank Mist They Draw": quotation from Milton's

Lycidas, a pastoral **elegy** (1637).

Terburg: Ter Borch, Gerard; Dutch painter (1617–1681).

Tergiversation: desertion of a cause, party or faith; shifting, evasion.

Thatch: covering for a roof, grain stack, etc., or to cover with straw, reeds, leaves, etc.

Thesmothete: from Athenian women who were judges and lawgivers, it has come to mean "one who lays down the law."

Thor: god of thunder - Norse or Scandinavian mythology.

Tophet: chaos, darkness, Hell.

Trochar: probe, stiletto - type instrument to insert drainage tube.

Turner, Joseph: English painter (1775–1851).

Turpin: famous eighteenth-century highwayman.

Vanity Of Human Wishes: meditative poem by Samuel Johnson (1709–1784).

Vega: star of the first magnitude, brightest star in constellation Lyra.

White Monday: day after Whitsunday (Pentecost); usually a bank holiday.

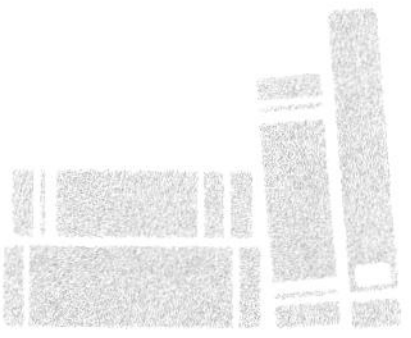

BIBLIOGRAPHY

Paperbound editions of *Far From the Madding Crowd*, with helpful critical material are available:

Hardy, Thomas. *Far From the Madding Crowd*. Carl J. Weber, editor, Holt-Rinehart-Winston. Introduction by Bergen Evans. Premier Books. Richard L. Purdy, editor. Riverside Editions. Afterword by James Wright. Signet Classics.

STUDIES OF HARDY'S LIFE AND WORKS

Abercrombie, Lascelles. *Thomas Hardy: A Critical Study*. London, 1912, 1964.

Babb, Howard. "Setting and **Theme** in *Far From the Madding Crowd*," *English Literary History*, XXX (1963), 147–161.

Beach, Joseph Warren. *The Technique of Thomas Hardy*. Chicago, 1922.

Blunden, Edmund. *Thomas Hardy*. London, 1941.

Brennecke, Ernest. *The Life of Thomas Hardy*. New York, 1925.

Brown, Douglas. *Thomas Hardy*. London, New York, 1954.

Carpenter, Richard C. "The Mirror and the Sword: **Imagery** in *Far From the Madding Crowd*," *Nineteenth Century Fiction*, XVIII (1964), 331–45.

Cecil, Lord David. *Hardy the Novelist*. London, 1960.

Chase, Mary Ellen. *Thomas Haidy from Serial to Novel*. Minneapolis, 1927.

Chew, Samuel. *Thomas Hardy: Poet and Novelist*. New York, 1928.

Duffin, Henry C. *Thomas Hardy: A Study of the Wessex Novels*. Manchester, 1927.

Elliot, A. P. *Fatalism in the Works of Thomas Hardy*. Philadelphia, 1962, reprint.

Firor, Ruth A. *Folkways in Thomas Hardy*. Philadelphia, 1962, reprint.

Grimsditch, Herbert B. *Character and Environment in the Novels of Thomas Hardy*. London, 1925.

Guerard, Albert J. *Thomas Hardy: Novels and Stories*. Cambridge, Mass., 1962.

______. ed., *Hardy: Collection of Critical Essays*, Englewood Cliffs, N.J., 1963.

Hardy, Eveln. *Thomas Hardy: A Critical Biography*. London, New York, 1949.

Hardy, Florence E. *Early Life of Thomas Hardy*, 1840–91. London, 1928.

______. *Later Years of Thomas Hardy*, 1892–1928. London, 1930.

Harper, C. G. *The Hardy Country: Literary Landmarks of the Wessex Novels*. 1904, 1911, 1925. Hawkins, Desmond. *Thomas Hardy*. London, 1950.

Hyde, W. J. "Hardy's View of **Realism**: A Key to the Rustic Characters." *Victorian Studies*, II (1958), 45–59.

Kettle, Arnold. *An Introduction to the English Novel.* II. London, 1961.

Lea, Hemann. *Thomas Hardy's Wessex.* London, 1913.

Macdowall, A. S. *Thomas Hardy: A Critical Study*. London, 1931.

Parker, W. M. "The Jubilee of *Far From the Madding Crowd*," *Cornhill Magazine*, LVI (1924).

Purdy, Richard L. *Thomas Hardy: A Bibliographical Study*. London, New York, Toronto, 1954.

Rutland, W. R. *Thomas Hardy: A Study of His Writings and Background*. New York, 1962.

Saxelby, F. O. *Thomas Hardy Dictionary*. New York, n. d.

Weber, Carl J. *Hardy of Wessex: His Life and Literary Career*. New York, 1940.

———. Colby *Notes on Far From the Madding Crowd*, Waterville, Maine, 1935.

Wing, George. *Thomas Hardy*. New York. Evergreen Pilot Edition, 1963.

Lightning Source UK Ltd.
Milton Keynes UK
UKHW020640051120
372844UK00012B/517